Ayrton Senna

The Messiah of Motor Racing

Richard Craig

DARTON · LONGMAN + TODD

First published in 2012 by
Darton, Longman and Todd Ltd
1 Spencer Court
140–142 Wandsworth High Street
London SW18 4JJ

ISBN 978-0-232-52910-4

A catalogue record for this book is available from the British Library.

Phototypeset by Kerrypress Ltd, Luton, Bedfordshire
Printed and bound by Bell & Bain, Glasgow

For my parents, Evan and Susan

Contents

Acknowledgments

First of all, I extend my thanks to my publisher Will Parkes for his faith in me and for giving me an opportunity that, in fairness, most writers wouldn't get if they tried for a hundred years.

Massive thanks must also go to Mike Doodson, whose company, insight, hearty Sussex grub and conversation on the merits of old Volkswagens was hugely appreciated.

I am also indebted to Thierry Boutsen and Keith Sutton for granting me a slot in their hectic schedules, and for giving me valuable material for this book.

The archives of *Autosport* magazine, particularly the work of their erstwhile Grand Prix editor Nigel Roebuck, have been indispensable. His forthright, irreverent and always entertaining opinions have been a staple part of my F1 diet since I was a schoolboy.

Finally, my heartfelt thanks to family and friends: Marianne for all her encouragement and for listening to endless whinging during the writing process; to my family, Mum, Dad, Phil and Jenny, for well, being my family.

To Phil, Dom and Ryan for proofreading and advice. And to Helen Porter, Managing Editor at DLT Books, for helping sift through endless re-reads.

Prologue

When I was ten years old, I borrowed a cartridge for my Nintendo Game Boy from a chap across the road. It was called something along the lines of *F1 Pole Position* and, in spite of the graphics being more reminiscent of green Lego bricks than Formula 1 cars, it was very good fun. It also enjoyed licensed status, using the drivers' real names. No doubt Nintendo funded Bernie's new conservatory with that deal.

Unlike other lads my age, I didn't seem to be able to master the game within ten seconds of sliding the power switch and was routinely beaten in every Grand Prix by my computer-generated opposition.

As I slipped into what I imagine was supposed to be a gravel trap for the umpteenth time, the game would put me out of my misery by ending the race and displaying a pixellated results board on screen.

There was only ever one name at the top: 'Senna.'

I didn't know a huge amount about Formula 1 at this stage: although thanks to my cursory glances at Grand Prix during previous years I thought Nigel Mansell was the be-all and end-all at the wheel of his Williams-Renault.

However, there was something intangibly exotic and mysterious about this foreign name. Above all, I knew this man was quick. Even in Nintendo-land, he was winning everything.

Then, one bank holiday weekend I was away with my family on a mini-break. As I came in from a frenetic cycle to fetch a glass of water, my mother said to me, 'Have you heard of Ayrton Senna?'

Of course I had.

'He's had a big crash in the Grand Prix and he's not well at all.'

When I returned home the next day my greatest rival in Nintendo world was no longer a man of our own. Somehow I didn't have the heart to play the game any more, so I took out the cartridge, walked across the road, and handed it back.

Part One

1

The Man Dies, The Myth Begins

'And here we are with Michael Schumacher … and Senna! My goodness! Senna has joined Pedro Lamy and JJ Lehto in a smashed motor car. What happened there I do not know …'

Murray Walker, commentating for BBC's *Grand Prix* programme, is as surprised as anyone when, in front of the Benetton-Ford's on-board camera the leading Williams suddenly darts off the track and ricochets against the trackside wall.

Bits of blue and white carbon-fibre fly everywhere as the car veers back into the path of those behind, all piling through the flat out left-hand Tamburello sweep. It then crawls back towards the gravel and stops, right-hand wheels ripped off along with most of the bodywork. There are scattered cheers from up in the grandstands as Ayrton Senna's elimination promotes the *tifosi*'s beloved Gerhard Berger to second place.

At home in Portugal, Senna's girlfriend Adriane Galisteu is also cheered by the exit. 'Oh good, he'll be home early', she thinks to herself.

For the third race in a row, the caption at the bottom of the TV screens shows that car number 2 is no longer involved in proceedings for the afternoon. Having spun into retirement in Brazil and been punted off the track at the first corner of the previous round in Aida, the world championship favourite has still not added a single point to his 1994 account – his worst ever start to a season.

Now elevated to third place, Damon Hill drives past his teammate's crumpled car and thinks to himself, 'Wow, not again. Ayrton's having a rotten season.'

For a few brief moments there is little concern for the Brazilian, as cars have suffered more spectacular accidents at the corner, and at other circuits in previous years and their pilots have emerged unscathed from their vehicles. Nelson Piquet, Michele Alboreto and Gerhard Berger to name three.

Berger's 1989 crash, despite triggering an apocalyptic fireball, left him with injuries so minor, considering what could have happened, he only needed to miss one race. So this latest crash, relatively tame in comparison, should pose Senna no problems, surely?

Senna seems in no rush to get out of the car. On the TV camera's long shot, it is unclear what he might be doing, although his helmet is definitely slumped over to one side. Perhaps he is winded, or talking to the team on the radio to apologise for what has happened. He might even have been knocked out.

As the helicopter hovers overhead, filming the wreckage of the FW16, Senna's head perceptibly moves, leading Walker's co-commentator Jonathan Palmer to express some brief hope that his former colleague is all right. But he is not all right. Although nobody was to know at that precise moment, we would never see the famous yellow crash helmet again. There was one notable exception – five-time champion and racing legend Juan Manuel Fangio, watching at home on television, got up and switched off his set. The maelstrom that was Ayrton Senna da Silva's 34-year life was no more.

Erik Comas, the Frenchman for whose safety Senna had risked his own life two years previous at Spa-Francorchamps, pulled over in his Larousse-Ford to see if there was anything he could do to return the favour. He saw the Brazilian's limp body on the stretcher, the medical team working full pelt to try and

...nd in the trap. That was ...on. With a horrible feeling of ...not be able to talk about for a further ten ...as returned to the pits and wasn't seen again for the ...st of the weekend.

Challenging the Legend

If you put the question, 'Who is Ayrton Senna?' to most people on the street, they'd probably, as Jeremy Clarkson acknowledges, say 'That F1 driver who died'.

Indeed, in 2009 Kevin Eason wrote in the *Times* that 'Ayrton Senna has been elevated to the status of a legend as much because of the dramatic circumstances of his death in front of a worldwide television audience [as his driving].'

And therein lies the reason I chose the title *The Messiah of Motor Racing* for my study of the triple world champion.

John Bisignano, an American journalist who interviewed Senna many times during a 15-year career working for ESPN as an F1 correspondent, says: 'For all those people in Brazil, for all his fans around the world, he will always be young. He will always be fast, never be old. He will always be the champion of Brazil and of the world. The grief, even today, is maybe the greatest statement I can make about what he did. Can you imagine hearing a news report, "Ayrton Senna dies of cancer at the age of 50"? I don't know. In some poetic way it was almost fitting that he died in a race car.'

There is definitely something messianic about him. He came, he trail-blazed, he ruffled feathers, he was loved by some, hated by others, and he died a public death when he was only a man in his early thirties.

Was Senna motorsport's messiah? And did he die so others might live?

His death led to the adoption of safety measures that arguably saved the lives of drivers including Jos Verstappen, Pedro Diniz, Alex Wurz, Luciano Burti, Mark Webber and many more. Meanwhile, the charitable foundation, *Instituto Ayrton Senna*, set up after his death has enriched the lives of thousands of poor children in his native Brazil.

Or, on the other hand, was he just a very naughty boy?

He certainly exhibited some thoroughly unsavoury habits – nearly always in the heat of competition – that could have endangered the lives of not only himself and his fellow drivers but marshals and spectators.

In truth, he was a bit of both, and many others besides. If there was ever a celebrity that deserved the tag 'enigma' it was Ayrton Senna da Silva.

Indeed, the *Senna* documentary of 2010 deserves huge praise and achieved what many would have thought difficult: it brought motor racing, and particularly Senna himself, to a mainstream audience. It is much like Martin Scorsese's *The Last Waltz,* which made the story of The Band's final concert fascinating whether or not you liked the Southern bluegrass music they largely played.

Of course it has both rekindled the interest of those who were aware of Senna's story already and ignited the attention of those who otherwise consider motor racing to be a cure for insomnia. A compelling story is a compelling story, regardless of the genre in which it is slotted.

Senna's influence has now grown far beyond the men and women who spent most of their weekends in the 1980s watching his exploits from their armchairs.

The British comedian Noel Fielding, a man whose unbridled televisual weirdness could not be further from the intense world of motor racing, explains what he felt after watching the film.

> Can you be in love with a dead racing driver? I watched the *Senna* documentary and I just thought he was amazing:

insanely good and completely single-minded, but also really enigmatic and spiritual. Everyone in this country's quite frightened by spirituality. In South America they talk a lot about being guided by a force, which makes us panic: 'What force? What did it look like? Was it wearing a hat? Who do I phone up to get my own force?' Senna's like a modern-day hero. His racing was almost like an act of poetry because it was so extreme.

The Observer's Paul Hayward, meanwhile, had this to say:

[Documentaries such as *Senna*] return us to the pre-corporate age when sport was a means of expression and not a branch of business. When Ayrton Senna defends himself as a pure 'racer', who drove against other men and their machines there is a subconscious pull to another time, before Formula 1 was a game of computer technology and industrialised product-shifting.

He was answering not to a series of commercial opportunities but a compulsion to race, to subjugate his contemporaries, starting with his main rival in a more glamorous era, Alain Prost.

An implication from *Senna* … is that sport works best not in the frenzied present moment but in memory, where it deepens and gains richness.

Back then, the cars were screaming monsters that had to be manhandled round bumpy tracks while the onboard cameras were shaken about as though they were attached to a jack-hammer. One of the driver's hands was on the wheel and the other on the gear lever. Yes, a gear lever. The steering wheels looked like steering wheels, not a cross between an iPad and a

PlayStation controller, and there were three pedals in the foot-well. We had everything from fire-breathing four-cylinder turbos to howling V12s. In the 1980s, if a driver was furious with another driver, he walked up to him and told him about it in no uncertain terms, and then told the press and the crowd over the circuit's PA system while he was at it. Compare and contrast the emotional intensity of Senna sitting down in front of the micro-phone after the dramatic qualifying session at Jerez in 1990, with the typical commercialised ramblings of a press conference in 2012. You would be hard pressed to find a video of a press conference in which Senna opens with 'I'd like to thank Honda Marlboro McLaren'.

It was a different time back then.

And yet *Senna* excelled at perpetuating the myth rather than telling us everything we wanted to know about the man.

There is a reason for all of this, of course: the film was made with the co-operation, and under the watchful eye of the Senna family, and was always going to verge on the hagiographic.

And it is arguable that this approach to appraising Senna's life has infiltrated the memories of many.

Mark Hughes is as forthright a Formula 1 journalist as you'll find, and he opened *Autosport's* superb Senna tribute last year with 'Even trying to write a balanced assessment of Ayrton Senna can draw you into a trough of eulogy or dysology, love or hate; it's near impossible to balance on the fence – the force-field of his persona lasers through the years to push you one side or the other.'

So, many do indeed wax lyrical about him with frequent recourse to superlatives and absolutes. An example of such can be found in a leading Senna biography in which the author says, succinctly, 'Senna never cruised, never backed off, never settled for what fate had given him that afternoon,' a statement that actually would be probably better applied to a driver like Gilles Villeneuve, who really did not.

Villeneuve took his never-give-up philosophy to levels that could be almost considered moronic – when he trailed his Ferrari back to the pits at Zandvoort in 1979, leaving sparks and bits of car in his wake, or drove with his front wing bent up into his line of vision, in the driving rain in Montreal in 1981.

Senna, was far too intelligent a racer to drive his 141 Grands Prix 100% flat-out all the time.

He said it himself: 'I don't care how strong or fit the driver; you can't drive flat out the whole distance.'

He was undoubtedly a man with an exceptional talent for driving racing cars. But let us all remember this is all he was. It is a very human tendency to only concentrate on what was positive about a person after they have died, especially if it is premature and most particularly if they are famous. Fame has the tendency to act as a metaphorical muscle suit that grows in size as their celebrity escalates, rather like the episode of *The Simpsons* in which Mr Burns decides to portray himself as a god by donning a physique-enhancing costume. It soon accidentally catches fire, and as it melts away he is left writhing on the ground, exposed as a human as frail and as mortal as he ever was.

'What's it like to be a racing driver?' Nelson Piquet was once asked.

'I still wake up in the morning, I am hungry to eat, and I fart. Just like everyone else.'

Racing drivers, in their displays of unbending nerve and breathtaking speed, convince the mere mortals eating hotdogs in the grandstand or drinking tea in the comfort of their living rooms that they are somehow different from them. And they are: not everybody could do what they do. But they aren't gods. They are supremely talented individuals, as are NASA engineers and brain surgeons. It's just that the latter do not appear on Sky Sports every fortnight. With fame and the public display of superhuman talent comes a tendency to be labeled as something divine. Blues guitarist Eric Clapton gained the nickname 'God' as if to prove the point.

Senna was an intelligent man and he knew all this himself. One almost wonders what he would make of the panegyric nature of pretty much everything now written about him.

'We go into millions of homes by way of television and people feel close to us. But at the same time they are far, far away. They have no idea what we are really like. They dream of watching a race live or getting to see one of us and perhaps if they had the opportunity they would see that we are just people, that there is nothing magic.'

We should not forget that Senna, before he became an icon, was a scrawny, softly-spoken and poorly co-ordinated chap who had to live in a chilly little rented house in Norfolk and spend his free time playing slot machines in greasy spoons with his fellow Formula Ford drivers.

His life was just a life and needs no editorial gloss applied to it – the remarkable events stand up on their own merits and do not necessitate slow-motion film sequences and dramatic music. Senna's negative traits are likewise best considered as they are. Sad to say, but in order to decide for oneself what he was really like, it is necessary to adopt a hard-headed cynical approach at times to counteract the layers of sycophancy added to many biographies. Unfortunately much of the recorded material available of Senna's exploits dates from the years after his death.

That Senna was effortlessly charismatic is not in doubt, yet let us not adopt pink-hued ocular apparatus too quickly. There were dull drivers then, and there are charismatic drivers now. Whether Senna complemented his era of F1, or it complemented him, it was a very different epoch. For the first four, and final two full seasons of his career he was not in title-winning cars and yet he was always there or thereabouts. And when he was in decent equipment, things were never easy. The fly in the ointment was either Alain Prost or Nigel Mansell and Senna had to drive his Nomex socks off to beat them.

Even when he won the title, in '88, '90 and '91, he never dominated the season, which arguably actually enhances his reputation. There were no Schumacher-esque displays, winning the title an embarrassing two months early and costing Bernie three-quarters of his viewing figures.

Senna's three titles, won in the face of relative adversity, inferior machinery or the strong rivalry posed by a worthy adversary seem all the more resonant. The man himself said as much. A title that is won by a driver who lucks into the best cars and buggers off into the distance is undoubtedly, in this author's opinion, somewhat devalued. People say 'Formula 1's all in the car.' No-one ever said that for Senna. Even when he had the fastest car on the grid at his disposal in 1988 and 1989, he had a curly-haired Frenchman in an identical vehicle scoring as many, if not more, points as him and making life difficult.

If anything it is arguable that too much success breeds contempt. Senna won often enough to remind the world how brilliant he was, but not so often that people switched off their televisions in droves. Put it this way: Alain Prost, in terms of race wins, world championships and fastest race laps is significantly ahead of him (although he had three extra seasons to rack up those additional wins). But do the vast majority of the public care? Not really. If stats were everything, Gilles Villeneuve would be relegated to the same status as men like Rene Arnoux. Villeneuve was a man who recorded only two pole positions and six race victories. He was never world champion, whereas his rival Alan Jones was. But who has more caché with the F1 racing fan today? Similarly, compare Stirling Moss and Mike Hawthorn twenty years before. There is something besides mere numbers that makes the greats so special.

In numerous polls and surveys, conducted amongst fans and F1 insiders, Senna's name appears at the top, despite him statistically no longer being the 'best' driver in any sense: the greatest numbers of championships, wins, pole positions and fastest laps have all been eclipsed by Michael Schumacher.

Why is this?

'It's because he transcended the sport and his job, even before his death,' says Martin Brundle. 'I think because he became a global icon as well as a racing driver – and I don't think he put any effort into [becoming] that by the way, that's just the way he was because he wore his heart on his sleeve – and because he was clearly so successful, people could associate with him.'

'I think also he was pretty controversial and that kind of news always travels too.'

'Because he drove with such commitment and such emotion, and not a little controversy, he was well known and ended up transcending the sport. I was thinking about it as I was watching the *Senna* movie the other night. 'How did the bloke I'd be idly chit-chatting to at places like the Cadwell Park paddock end up being this international icon?'

In the ten years since he had burst on to the Grand Prix scene with his unforgettable drive at Monaco in 1984, Formula 1 fans had seen Senna achieve the breathtaking, as well as perpetrate the unthinkable, with each season he spent in the sport merely adding to his allure. Even when, during qualifying for the 1991 Mexican Grand Prix, his car somersaulted into the tyre wall at Peraltada, he remained unscratched, although he was bearing a nasty gash on his head from a jet-skiing accident.

Partly thanks to F1's increasing complacency, he seemed immortal, a man possessed of such God-given talents, not to mention a passionate and unashamedly public connection with their progenitor, that it was easy to forget that something as simple as a car crash could deprive the world of him.

In 2010 veteran motorsport journalist Mike Doodson wrote, in *Motor Sport:* 'One day, somebody will write a great full-length biography of Ayrton Senna da Silva. Let's hope it won't take a couple of centuries for that someone to compile the balanced, well-informed assessment of the Brazilian's 34-year life.'

What he was alluding to is the absolute, unyielding respect and sometimes borderline blandishment with which the Senna myth is treated.

'I think [this phenomenon] is entirely to be expected,' he told me. 'When somebody is dead you can write about him in ways that you didn't before. You can be more critical, or more fulsome about his qualities. There is some hagiography surrounding Senna because some people regarded him as superhuman, which clearly he wasn't. They put that into words and it's a bit embarrassing to read what they write.

'Others balance it out by pointing out the counterpoint: the ruthlessness and so forth, which has spread through F1. In my opinion and in that of many others this has been a bad influence.'

The public like their heroes to swash as many buckles as possible and if their fanaticism requires them to accept a dollop of maverick behaviour every now and again, so be it. Even if that maverick behaviour happens to involve directing carbon-fibre missiles into others at speeds in excess of 150mph.

It is a measure of the respect accorded to Senna that his displays of selfish single-mindedness, while doubtless frowned upon at the time, have become part of the story. The nature of films like *Senna* and the earlier documentary *A Star Named Ayrton Senna* fall into the trap of treating celebrities who have died with an almost cloying flattery and allows events such as the torpedoing of Alain Prost at the Japanese Grand Prix of 1990 to be painted as romantic, as a wronged star's only recourse to justice following the discrimination demonstrated against him by 'the system'.

It could be argued too many drivers have died or suffered serious injury following *accidental* crashes without deliberate collisions being added to the mix. There is a distinction to be drawn between ruthlessness and outright brazen selfishness or even stupidity.

As a case in point, Michael Schumacher has also been guilty of cheating and pushing the boundaries of acceptable behaviour in order to attain success throughout his career, and yet he has been demonized for it.

In an assessment of both drivers' careers, Senna is painted as the relentless hero, always on the limit and sometimes beyond, even in terms of his behaviour. Schumacher, although generally perpetrating 'accidents' at much lower speed than Senna and never truly putting anyone in real danger, is the man who sees himself denigrated far more regularly. Senna's actions are now part of his legend. Schumacher's behaviour, in contrast, is spoken of in terms of dislike to this day: Keke Rosberg once said of him, 'He is a cheap cheat. He should leave F1 to honest people.'

Apart from the fact that Senna is dead and Schumacher is not, it is hard to fathom a reason for this disparity, especially since Senna was indeed berated by journalists and fellow drivers during his career.

He himself admitted that nobody is perfect and while he was alive he was also aware that 'often I don't get the best press in England'. There were many reasons for this: yes, there was an element of jingoism as the mysterious Johnny Foreigner from Sao Paulo had the temerity to veto Derek Warwick and lock horns with Nigel Mansell, but also because Senna could be as unpleasant and duplicitous as anyone if he felt like it.

Death and celebrity

It is a cynical but undeniable truth that premature death enhances the reputation of a celebrity. Recent history is littered with examples of sportsmen, musicians and other public figures for whom an unscheduled meeting with their maker turns out to be the best career move they ever made, and whose legacy is enshrined as a result.

One would be hard pressed to find anyone grumbling that Jimi Hendrix was a guitarist no more talented than contemporaries like Eric Clapton, Jeff Beck or Jimmy Page, that Kurt Cobain was nothing special, that James Dean couldn't act his way out of a paper bag or that Elvis Presley turned into a greasy, bloated parody of himself in his later years, or that Steve Jobs was a ruthless and occasionally unpleasant boss who was merely excellent at marketing others' ideas.

Such viewpoints border on sacrilege. Indeed, in his book *Gods Behaving Badly,* Pete Ward argues that the fanaticism with which some celebrities, especially those who are unfortunately deceased, borders on religious fervour. For whatever reason an early death vacuum-seals a celebrity's legend, whilst simultaneously squeezing the more unsavoury elements of their personality out into the atmosphere. The public will never have to see their idols grow old and lose the aura that made them so special in the first place.

Take the example of the late Amy Winehouse. The jazz singer was berated by the British tabloids for living on a diet of hedonism and Haribo sweets, mocked for slurring her way through concerts and for setting a bad example to youngsters. Yet, when she died, as a result of that very lifestyle, the same papers that had kicked her to the ground time after time all lumped in together to build her a pedestal.

Diana, Princess of Wales, was treated with the same hypocritical reverence by the press who bestowed her with Tony Blair's title 'the people's princess' as a consolation for hounding her in the months before the Paris car crash that claimed her life.

At the time John Lennon was murdered, his musical output was stuttering and sporadic. Before *Double Fantasy,* in the shops only three weeks before his death, he had not released an album for five years having essentially disappeared from public life. John Peel said that *Double Fantasy* and *Milk and Honey* (released just after Lennon's death), 'weren't very good'.

And yet, when he was killed, he became a legend for the rest of time. Paul McCartney, is still playing twenty-six minute versions of *Hey Jude* at the age of 70 and is arguably a better musician than Lennon ever was, but because he has reached a certain age he will never have his former partner's immortal allure when he retires to the Cavern Club in the sky.

Photographer Keith Sutton, the founder of Sutton Motorsport Images, met Ayrton Senna when they were both in their early twenties, in 1981. He soon struck up a friendship with the determined young driver, as both men had ambitions to make it to Formula 1 in their own way. Keith recognises 'anyone who dies young is immortalised – Marilyn Monroe, Elvis, John Lennon. Obviously just recently with the [release of the] movie, there is a whole new generation learning about him.'

And of course in Formula 1 heroes had died in the pursuit of glory countless times before that black weekend at Imola in 1994.

The last driver to die at the wheel of a Formula 1 car had been the popular Italian Elio de Angelis in 1986. He was testing his troublesome Brabham BT55 at Paul Ricard in southern France when his rear wing failed. He landed upside down on the wrong side of the guard rail, the blue and white car bursting into flames. Due to the total lack of proper fire marshaling and medical facilities, his life was essentially thrown away for no good reason. His physical injuries were slight, but it was the noxious fumes from the flames that deprived him of oxygen and caused his death from catastrophic brain damage the next day.

De Angelis was, like Senna, a charismatic, talented and handsome young man from a privileged background. But most people outside F1 circles would be hard pushed to know who he was.

Gilles Villeneuve never approached Senna's levels of success. Yet he is nevertheless considered by many of those in the know to be the sport's most abundantly talented driver. While he often span off the track in his quest to find the car's limit (often some way below his own) he also recorded wins in recalcitrant machines that had no right to put their driver on the top step of the podium. When he did get his hands on competitive machinery, either luck was against him or his sense of honour, a flashback to gentlemen drivers of the 1950s, meant he ceded to his more consistent teammate in the title chase.

In some ways he is very like Senna. Former F1 doctor, Professor Sid Watkins, was good friends with both drivers and has often noted their similarity. Both men were held in awe by their peers and by fans alike for the levels of performance they could extract from themselves. At Monaco in 1981 Villeneuve qualified his ungainly tank of a Ferrari on the front row, the mirror opposite of where it belonged. His teammate had qualified on pole position for the same event the year before and was 2.478 seconds back. Not dissimilar to what would happen there seven years later when Senna thrashed Prost in qualification for the '88 event. Both men even raced with the same number for longer than any other: 12.

Meanwhile, 1982 was to be another one of those years. As with the death of Senna in 1994 at Imola, there was something of an ill wind blowing through the paddock at Zolder on May 8, 1982.

A week earlier at San Marino, Ferrari, unhindered by most of their rivals who had decided to stay at home thanks to the treatment they were receiving at the hands of Jean-Marie Balestre's autocratic FISA, had a demonstration run to the flag in their sights. There was a brief threat to victory for either Villeneuve or teammate Didier Pironi, in the shape of the two Renaults driven by Alain Prost and Rene Arnoux. True to form, however, they both politely took themselves out of contention before they could ruin the Italian spectators' picnic.

Villeneuve was now the team's number one driver, having played a support role to Jody Scheckter during the South African's title-winning year in 1979. In the closing stages of the race, with nothing to challenge them, the two Ferrari drivers were ordered to cool the pace.

Pironi, himself no slouch, zoomed up to the back of his teammate's now conservatively-driven car and promptly overtook him, to the Canadian's surprise. As Clive James so drily intones in his commentary for the official FIA review of that season, Pironi 'had a long think about whether he wanted to finish first or second, and decided he wanted to finish first'.

Believing his colleague was indulging in a bit of showmanship for the adoring crowd, Villeneuve played along, re-passing the Frenchman and being counter-attacked several times. What he didn't count on was Pironi screeching past on the final tour as Villeneuve left the door wide open at Tosa. The normally open and jovial little Canadian vowed never to speak to his erstwhile friend again.

With this evil atmosphere presiding at Zolder, he went out for qualifying and drove like a man possessed, so blinded by his determination to put Pironi in his place that Jochen Mass's Arrows, in trying to get out of his way, did the opposite and launched the Ferrari into the air. Villeneuve was flung from his disintegrating 126C2 in front of the TV cameras and the world of motorsport lost what James called 'a poet of a driver'.

Alberto Ascari is another legendary driver whose career and eerie death would arguably make an engrossing documentary.

Having totally dominated Grand Prix racing in the first two years that it was run to Formula 2 rules and specifications (1952 and 1953) he had, like Senna, spent two seasons without winning a championship as he was given outclassed machinery. During the 1955 Monaco Grand Prix he got it all wrong on lap 80 as he exited the tunnel and ended up crashing through the barriers and into the harbour, amazingly suffering only minor scuffs and a broken nose.

After his Monaco crash Ascari's lucky helmet, which was certainly living up to its reputation, had taken a bit of a knock but rather than replace it, he sent it to be repaired. Four days after

Monte Carlo he was back in action for Ferrari at Monza to test a new sportscar but without his headgear, obliging him to borrow his friend Eugenio Castellotti's.

On the the third lap, entering the corner that now bears his name, he crashed and was thrown out of the car and killed. Even more spine-tingling was the fact that his death came on 26th day of the month, at the age of 36, exactly as his father Antonio had passed away.

It is disingenuous to argue that Senna is only as famous as he is because he died so young: Villeneuve and de Angelis, and many others before them, perished prematurely and yet have not attained the status of international heroes. Senna was a star when he was alive, but it would be a brave commentator who would argue that he is not *quite* as legendary as he is because he died when he did.

His death not only sealed his status permanently, it also kick-started a thorough re-appraisal of the safety and wisdom of Grand Prix racing. In days gone by, safety improvements were only introduced at the behest of drivers like Jackie Stewart, who made himself a permanent thorn in the side of the powers-that-be until life-saving measures were introduced. Twenty-five years later, nobody needed to be told twice. In the now eighteen years since Senna's Imola crash, there has not been a single fatality at the wheel of a contemporary Grand Prix car, although sadly two marshals lost their lives at the start of the 2000s.

Jim Clark was the Senna of his day, essentially peerless, and a man of whom Senna himself was greatly enamoured. In seven seasons of racing, he won two championships and amassed 33 pole positions and 25 Grand Prix victories. His strike rates in terms of wins converted from pole positions and championships won in seasons contested are remarkably similar to Senna's. When he won in 1965, he amassed a perfect score, collecting 54 points out of the 54 available that counted, the only driver to ever achieve this feat.

He was sublime in the wet and was capable of thrashing the opposition in such conditions. He too died unnecessarily, at the wheel of a racing car. He was even younger than Senna, at 32.

Arguably it should be Clark who remains the ultimate hero of F1, the poster boy. Clark apparently had all of Senna's abilities and none of his foibles, the type of man who would have felt guilty for a week if he'd as much as spat a stone at a rival's paintwork as he overtook them.

While he was indubitably F1's megastar at the time, his was an era in which the Ecclestone juggernaut had not yet chugged into town with its all-encompassing TV coverage at every race. In 1968, Formula 1 was still the preserve of people who could actually be bothered to make the journey to a circuit, armed with windbreaks, picnic rugs and egg sandwiches and the occasional 8mm film camera. In other words, enthusiasts.

When Clark arrived at Hockenheim on April 7th, 1968, Formula 1 was still in its black and white era: a sport that had not yet developed into what it would become by the time of Senna's accident in 1994. Sponsorship was only just starting to filter into the sport and the cars were still devoid of wings and slick tyres, albeit not for much longer. Clark's last ever F1 win, at Kyalami in South Africa three months before, had also been the final race in which all the participant teams would compete without overt sponsorship decals. F1 was still a sport, one hundred per cent, as opposed to a business and a television spectacle as well.

When Clark died, it was in a relatively minor F2 race (albeit one well-attended by most Grand Prix drivers and teams) and the accident was not captured on film. His death was only reported by the newspapers the next morning and witnessed by no one except the people following him on the track. It was slightly reminiscent of the death of the great Northern Irish motorcycle racer Joey Dunlop in 2000, incongruously killed in a relatively minor race in Estonia in which he was competing for fun, at the height of his success.

Senna, by contrast, suffered his fatal accident in front of a global television audience of millions while he was in the lead of the race. His had the shock factor that pummelled his name into the consciousness of those people who had only a peripheral awareness of his existence before that, in a similar way to the tragic irony of Dan Wheldon, whose success was only retrospectively recognised in his native Britain when his death had put his name into the headlines. In 1994, for every racing fan who already knew who Senna was, there were five Joe Bloggses who discovered his identity via the news headlines on the evening of 1 May, 1994.

On that tragic day, the world watched as the medical team milled around the wreckage of his car. They were given up-to-the-minute soundbites on events as they became known. F1 fans had witnessed his death as it happened, and been reminded in real time and with horrible clarity that motor racing is a highly dangerous sport that doesn't discriminate between the greats and the backmarkers.

3

Ayrton the Man

Faith

Religion has always been part of my life, and has become more important in the last two years. It gives me the peace and the equilibrium that I need to perform under stress, under pressure, all the time. I have found through God a special way of living and understanding many things in life that I didn't have before I started to understand what God is all about.

There aren't many who would pretend Ayrton Senna wasn't a little bit different to most of his contemporaries. On the track, he was probably the best of his era but he wasn't utterly peerless.

Off-track, however, one way in which he stood miles apart from the Prosts, the Piquets and the Mansells was in his introduction of God to the world of Grand Prix racing.

God features in sport frequently enough. He doesn't participate actively, but he is at times rather prominent.

I remember watching a football match when I was a child with my father. Upon the netting of a crucial goal, the scorer wheeled away and looked to the sky, crossing himself. I asked my dad what he was doing.

'He's blessing himself.'

'What's that?'

'He's thanking God.'

'Why?'

'Because he scored a goal.'

'Does God care about football?'

'Well, this guy seems to think so.'

'But how come God is on his side and not on the other team?'

'He isn't.'

'I don't understand.'

Critics of Senna's religious beliefs often scoffed the same opinion.

'His form of Christianity doesn't sit with the form that I was taught,' opines Mike Doodson. 'I was told that all men are equal in the sight of God. Well, clearly Senna didn't go along with that.'

Perhaps God was keeping tabs on his investment: after all, it certainly seemed he had put more time into honing Senna's talent than many of the rest on the grid.

It is unusual for a racing driver to remark: 'It is my biggest wish to be able to understand a little better the way he has given us life: the sky, the moon, the earth, the sun, the animals, the human beings, the enormous universe that is out there, the unknown space we ignore.'

You can almost imagine the hacks all retorting, 'Isn't he just supposed to whinge about his gear ratios?'

Senna did say such things of course, but he had a tendency to come out with metaphysical whimsy that had jaws dropping behind the Dictaphones when all present were least expecting it.

His open admission of his deep religious faith merely served to underline the mysterious aura he exuded, and his serious demeanour in front of the flashbulbs didn't contradict it.

He was brought up in a Roman Catholic family but his was a more spiritual, fluid belief. He didn't really follow the tenets of Catholicism strictly. He rarely went to church, although this was understandable since he tended to be busy most weekends.

'I am able to experience God's presence on earth. If I go to church, I go on my own and I like to be there alone. I find more peace that way', he explained.

Mike Doodson says, 'I would say that it's a mistake to evaluate Senna's religious foibles on the basis of being Catholic. I don't think that he would have said that he was first and foremost a Catholic. He seemed to take something from various religions. I don't think this business of opening the Bible at any page is Catholic – I think it's more some kind of evangelical thing.'

Maybe so. From the very first minute he sat in Grand Prix machinery in July 1983, he was already setting out his stall to the TV cameras, telling them in helmet-muffled Portuguese 'I think God is giving me a gift for which I have been waiting a long time, and he is helping me to stay calm.'

By the time Senna had become a megastar, God was a prominent member of his entourage. The weekend at Monaco in 1988, in which he spoke of having out of body experiences during qualifying and then seeing God when he binned his car into the Armco the next day, were too much for some people.

'I am a religious man. I believe in God, through Jesus,' he said. 'I was brought up that way, was maybe drifting away from it, but suddenly turned the other way.'

At Suzuka he was once more relating tales, straight-facedly, of how he had witnessed God as he completed his first warm-down lap as the world champion. This again drew snorts of derision.

'What do you say about a man who says he's seen God in any circumstances, never mind on the last lap of a Grand Prix?' asks Senna biographer Richard Williams. 'Most people would be sceptical, and I think those people would be right.'

He does add, however: 'Senna seemed to be absolutely convinced that he'd seen God: he didn't say what God was, how God appeared to him, but it's his right to say that. He must have known that he would risk attracting scepticism. And who are we to challenge that?'

What sat uneasily with some people was the form Senna's faith took. Although his considerable altruism, both in terms of personal donations to charity and his indirect establishment of the *Instituto Ayrton Senna*, became apparent after his death, the general consensus during his lifetime was that Senna's brand of spirituality seemed to be more about him than anyone else, and he wasn't particularly humble with it.

One of the critics of this openness was, unsurprisingly, Alain Prost, who seemed unnerved by it all. He preferred to keep his religious affairs private and memorably once said, 'Ayrton has a small problem – he thinks that because he believes in God he cannot kill himself.'

'I believe in God too, but I never used the same words that Ayrton did,' he later revealed. 'These kind of things do not make you very comfortable because it's like using that as a strength and thinking he was always right, and it could be dangerous on the track.'

Yet Senna knew that he could be killed as easily as anyone else.

'It hurts me if things come out such as I have a feeling that I am unbeatable or even immortal because of my belief in God.

'Just because I believe in God, just because I have faith in God, it doesn't mean that I'm immune. It doesn't mean that I'm immortal.

'There is a great difference between faith and the fear of death or getting hurt.

'What I said was that God gives me strength, but also that life is a present that God has given to us and that we are obliged to keep it, to handle it carefully.'

Former F1 driver Thierry Boutsen was a great friend of Senna's and has expressed the opinion that this ignorance was one of the greatest problems for Senna in his professional and personal dealings saying he 'was most affected by the words of people who did not try to understand him'.

Yet Prost had a point. Racing drivers are intrinsically a selfish bunch. They have to be. Even 'nice guys' like Johnny Herbert and Derek Warwick still want to see themselves out-achieve their rivals. Racers have through the decades, employed every tool at their disposal to achieve this aim. Outright talent for driving a car quickly is even more useful when combined with psychological warfare and a healthy sprinkling of subterfuge.

'I have had all my life very strong and good education, and from that I have got clear and strong principles and way of behaving,' Senna said in 1990. 'I use those guidelines to move as a man, as a professional and I don't regret anything. I just feel that I am doing things for the right reasons, some understand, some don't. You will never get everybody to agree and accept. Most of them admire, after all, what I'm doing as a professional, as a man, as many drivers do. We are exposing our lives there consistently. The reason for it is only one: is to succeed. To win, to get the thrill when you cross the finish line in first place.'

Senna was a great man but not necessarily a nice or a particularly popular one: he openly admitted to being, in his own words, 'a b*****d' after Nigel Mansell beat him to the 1992 drivers' title and was known for keeping himself to himself. But he had to be like this: when was the last time a lovely bloke won three F1 championships?

Racers are also, in many cases, hypocrites. They expect unwavering support and yet denigrate others who expect the same treatment. Ayrton Senna was guilty of hypocrisy at several key points during his ten seasons in Formula 1, as I will discuss in more detail, another aspect of his personality that seemed to deviate slightly from the Christian ideal. Doodson says 'The thing is that Senna believed that different standards applied to him than those that applied to other people. I think this is reflected to some extent in this religious thing he professed.' This is something that Prost has also drawn attention to.

After the toughness of 1989 and 1990 Senna's ease at discussing his faith faltered a great deal. Following the controversial end to both seasons, where he felt many within the press were against him, Senna seems to have decided to leave God out of proceedings.

Martin Donnelly, who was greatly touched by Senna's reaction to his sickening, career-ending accident at Jerez in 1990, says, 'Unfortunately for him, the British tabloids jumped on [his religiousness] and said "he's a Bible basher, he believes in God", just because he couldn't explain the experiences he felt, and no one would understand. That's why Ayrton started to distance himself from the press. He had his own beliefs, and he ended up with his own small group that he would speak to in the press – those that took him seriously as a driver – and the rest he wouldn't give the time of day for.'

Ron Dennis adds, 'There were many cynics in Formula 1 who challenged whether this was really an authentic and real account of what he felt and what his values were. But I was there to witness it, very often, in a more private environment, and he was most definitely sincere. He felt he was supported by the God that he believed in, and why on earth would I dissuade him from that belief? Strong beliefs are a good thing as long as they're positive.'

Ironically, after Senna decided to keep his own counsel with God, perhaps his most Christian actions occurred.

He once said: 'everything has a reason and only God knows the harmony of the universe. His will, his motivation, his reasons, he only understands'.

Ron Dennis again remembers in the days after Senna's death, he found himself feeling strangely uncomfortable as he realised that, in his view at least, Senna would not have done a thing differently, even if he knew he must die at an early age. The man himself had said, with fateful prescience: 'I want to live fully, very intensely. I would never want to live partially, suffering from illness or injury. If I ever happen to have an accident that eventually costs my life, I hope it happens in one instant.'

Humanity

Whatever reservations were aired in public or held in private with regard to Senna's open and devout religious conviction, displays of his humanity toward his fellow drivers on at least two notable occasions drew nothing but respect from all corners.

The events in Friday qualifying for the Spanish Grand Prix of 1990 had a sobering outcome on the whole Grand Prix fraternity, but most publicly the man from Sao Paulo.

Northern Ireland's Martin Donnelly suffered a suspected suspension failure as he rounded the right-hand bend behind the Jerez pits. He was launched in a sickening crash that tore off the front of his car and flung him across the circuit, leaving him lying in the middle of the track like a discarded puppet, the remains of his seat still strapped to his back and his legs bent at horrific angles.

Doodson remembers it as 'the most horrible accident I ever saw. I remember ringing my office and saying, 'Clear a page for an obituary'.

Italian Pierluigi Martini, driving for Minardi that day and the first on the scene, parked his car to protect Donnelly from other drivers on hot laps, as did Nelson Piquet. They and many to subsequently arrive were convinced their colleague was dead. The medical team, led by Sid Watkins, were on the scene swiftly to attend to the stricken driver. That his legs were badly broken was clear for all to see, but that was the least of anyone's worries.

Senna, not for the last time, commissioned a circuit car to take him to the accident scene and watched closely as the medical team performed an emergency tracheotomy on Donnelly and massaged his still heart back into life.

Prof Watkins, in an interview he gave to Nigel Roebuck in 1998, admits that he couldn't decide whether it was beneficial or detrimental for the drivers to take such close interest in the misfortune of one of their fellow practitioners. Although clearly shaken, Senna took a keen interest in the various procedures, filing them away in his mind for future use. His efforts would not be in vain.

Donnelly, a jovial character who admits he was just grateful to be a Grand Prix driver, was very different to the ruthless Brazilian in many ways. His promising career was over and he, limited by uncompetitive machinery, had not even so much as scored a point in Formula 1.

The two had come to know each other many years before as former Van Diemen drivers killing time at the famous Ed's Café near Snetterton, 'eating with the mechanics and playing Space Invaders'.

In an interview he later gave to former *Autosport* editor Andy Hallbery, the Ulsterman said 'Ayrton saw it all first-hand, holding my crash helmet and possibly watching me die on the track. Then he went back to his garage, put his helmet back on, visor down, and went and did the fastest lap of Jerez ever at the time.'

In the press conference after qualifying, Senna walked in to the throng of waiting journalists, and without even being asked a question, began to speak:

> Today is an unbelievable achievement … after yesterday's accident with Donnelly which was very sad for all of us. As you know I went to the place where he was on the ground and when I saw the consequences of the incident by myself with my eyes it was very difficult to cope with it, to maintain balance, to understand, to absorb it, to go forward from there. I felt like not running all of yesterday, from the moment I saw the incident there, I had some minutes on my own, quiet, in the motorhome, and I was able to go through very special moments there, getting everything inside of me. As I went on I did an amazing lap yesterday, it was unbelievable under the circumstances.

As much as I can try to express my feelings, I don't think anybody will ever be able to understand what I felt yesterday after the incident ... and when I went into it, the way I drove, the way I looked at it, the way I approached it, the way I experienced it is not something I can express in any way.

Thierry Boutsen, driving for Williams that day, told me: 'We had been all shocked by the accident; it was a huge reminder to all of us that we do a dangerous sport and need to respect this. Ayrton and I did not discuss this at the time, only later but very briefly. As drivers these are things you live with and accept but have difficulty talking about.

'Although it seemed the opposite, mainly to people who did not know him, Senna was a racing driver with brain and feelings, he cared about all his colleagues like if they were all his brothers.'

Donnelly eventually made a very good recovery, although to this day his feet, badly broken in the crash, require ongoing attention and he is obliged to wear orthopaedic shoes. This did not deter him from setting up a racing academy at Snetterton and, in July 2011, he got back behind the wheel of a Type 102 Lotus at the Goodwood Festival of Speed, drily saying of the car that nearly killed him, 'It's a bit like an old girlfriend, you fall out with it 20 years ago and it keeps coming back to bother you.'

The techniques Senna had observed from the 'Prof' that day did not go to waste. Two years later at Spa-Francorchamps, Senna was perfectly placed to help another fellow driver in need.

Frenchman Erik Comas, driving for Ligier, was participating in free practice when he crashed and was knocked unconscious:

'Ayrton basically saved my life at Spa in 1992', Comas told *Autosport* many years later. 'The weekend before the GP was the Spa 24 hours and they had removed the inside curve at Blanchimont and forgotten to put it back for F1. After only three laps of free practice JJ Lehto put dirt and gravel all over the track. I was just seconds behind and went off. I had an accident just like Ayrton's [at Imola]. The right front wheel hit my helmet and knocked me out. All the cars passed my car, including my teammate [Thierry Boutsen, incidentally], but Ayrton heard that my engine was still running, stopped and turned the master switch off. After that we had a close relationship.'

Senna also held Comas' head still in order that he would not be further injured if he had hurt his neck. Sid Watkins remembers: 'By the time I got there, Senna was kneeling down, holding his neck – in the correct way, I might add. As we took over, Ayrton said, "I made sure his breathing was all right, and I've asked the marshal to keep the helmet, so you can examine it for damage." He was a great student. Never forgot a thing.'

The footage of Senna scrambling out of his McLaren and running through the clouds of smoke to the stricken Ligier is stirring stuff to say the least. Although relegated to the closing credits of the *Senna* film, this, as much as anything, tells you what was best about the man.

Patriotism

No matter how famous Senna became, one element of his life remained a constant was his love of both Brazil, and the people there.

Mike Doodson, knew Senna personally and made many visits to Brazil during his longer career as Grand Prix correspondent.

'Unless you've been to Brazil you can't appreciate its importance to a Brazilian. There's some poetry in their soul. The food and the music and the atmosphere all comes together and it's absolutely irresistible,' he asserts.

Senna was greatly influenced by his family and especially his father, who had funded his early motor racing career and had a say in many things his eldest son did. But Milton da Silva was no autocratic cane-wielder and the mutual affection between him and Ayrton was evident throughout the Senna's racing career: Milton's attempted steering of his son's affairs was borne of protectiveness and nothing else.

Senna never thought twice about fleeing to Brazil when he had a spare moment in his schedule, and it is seemingly the only place he ever truly relaxed. Watch any archive footage of him holidaying with his family, or even being interviewed by Brazilian TV, and he is a different man. Whereas his most intense stares, prolonged silences and brooding answers were reserved for European journalists and television cameras, Senna was often to be found smiling broadly and gabbling away like anyone else when he was on home soil, revealing something of his Latin side. In Portuguese, he didn't have to watch what he said.

We know Senna was totally devoted to his racing and on several occasions described motorsport as 'my hobby as well as my profession'.

But it was, nonetheless still a job. An arduous and dangerous job that required constant travel, scrutiny and political nous. With this in mind, it was no wonder that Senna could often feel weighed down by the pressures of work, and there can be little doubt family and home were unquestionably the most important things to him.

He told Denis Jenkinson of his lack of enthusiasm at Spa in 1990, when there were virtually as many starts as competing drivers: 'When I saw the red flag come out for the second time, I had to suppress a desire to jump out of the car and walk away for the rest of the afternoon.'

In his McLaren days, while he supped fruit juice on a Brazilian beach, willing sidekick Gerhard Berger (and before that the much-less-willing Alain Prost) pounded the test track in the new car. Only when Senna felt ready would he eventually return, just in time to reward his teammate's long hours of hard work by thrashing him in qualifying for the first race. Prost and Berger had what one might call a thankless task.

In Malcolm Folley's excellent *Senna Versus Prost,* Prost himself remembers being asked at the start of 1989 to undertake the lion's share of the pre-season testing as Senna offered a plethora of excuses to Ron Dennis to explain his non-attendance.

'I'd had two weeks holiday and he was doing nothing for three months. I felt we had different jobs. Ayrton started the test, but after half a day in the car he said to Ron he didn't want to test any more. I was stupid enough to do the test [instead] and when I had the car how we wanted Ayrton came back and said he wanted to drive again.'

On top of Senna's relationship with the country itself, there was his regard for its people, and their regard for him.

The South American country is home to some of the most staggeringly beautiful scenery on earth, and yet the most heart-wrenching poverty. Senna had grown up in a privileged enclave of Sao Paulo and had never wanted for anything, but as he grew older he became aware of what had been happening the whole time outside the glass-topped perimeter walls of his family home.

Senna's health guru, Josef Leberer, was a man who was closer to him than most. On one car journey in the country he took a long look at the urban decay around him and asked Senna if he was ever bothered by the squalor and suffering around him. 'I'm not strong enough to do anything about it', was the reply.

He was right, of course. One man can't make a great difference and Senna knew that only the politicians could do anything worthwhile about it. But that didn't stop him trying. After his death it was revealed that he had donated millions of pounds to charity. He had staunchly refused to talk about his altruism when he was alive. This is probably what Frank Williams meant when he said that Senna was an even greater man out of the cockpit than in it.

Sid Watkins also tells a story of visiting Senna in Brazil, in which the two of them were going out for a walk and Senna was recognised by a group of children. He took his time to talk to them and didn't shoo them away.

That Senna is a megastar in his homeland is not in doubt. There are, however, some who take a slightly sceptical view.

In 2007, social anthropologist Dr Joaquim Diegues told *The Telegraph*:

> It is true that to the white upper-middle class he was one of our great sporting heroes. Not as popular as Pele, maybe, but as beloved as our other great football stars. But if you ignore Brazil's middle class – which represents only about two per cent of our people – then his popularity today is even more remarkable.

> The poor black children of the *favelas* do not dream of becoming Ayrton Senna. No, they still dream of being Pele or Zico or, more recently, Ronaldinho. Most of these children will never learn to drive, so for them motor racing is not a religion.

> Senna was always careful to present himself to the Brazilian people as a great patriot. He carried the flag of Brazil on his victory lap, for example. An image which is still being carefully polished by his family and business executives.

> His birthday, anniversary of his death and each Brazilian Grand Prix inspires another outpouring of grief, but though three million Brazilians lined the streets of Sao Paulo on the day of his funeral many, many more millions had never heard of Senna until he died at the age of 34.

This may be surprising to some, but Dr Diegues goes on:

> Our greatest talent lies not on the dance floor, the football stadium or in staging the carnival. Perhaps no

other country can match our talent for national mourning. That is why you have seen for yourself how Ayrton Senna has become more important in death than he ever was in life.

In contrast, a feature in the news magazine *Veja* said:

'Brazilians have this irreverence towards their idols. They laughed about the Emperor Pedro I's lovers, laughed again whenever [singer and composer] Tom Jobim got drunk or when Pele referred to himself in the third person. The only exception is Ayrton Senna. Brazilians worship Ayrton much the same way the Argentines do [king of tango] Carlos Gardel and Evita Peron.'

I asked Mike Doodson, as a man who saw Senna's impact first-hand, for his opinion on Dr Diegues's thoughts.

'When Senna was alive every Brazilian paper had a GP correspondent so you'd be making a mistake to downplay the importance of him to the Brazilian nation. There are visitors to his grave every day. I think he's probably on the same sort of level as Pele.'

Indeed the visitors to Senna's grave outnumber those of John F. Kennedy, Marilyn Monroe and Elvis Presley combined, so perhaps this tells you all you need to know.

Humour

It has been widely acknowledged that Senna had a reputation as being somewhat serious and dour, and while it may be true to say he didn't like to be making fun when he was preparing to go racing, is it insensitive to say he was humourless?

Autosport's edition from 5 May 1994, carries poignant tributes to both Senna and Roland Ratzenberger, including a photo montage of the Brazilian at key moments in his career. Whilst leafing through this precious magazine, there is one photo that strikes the observer: a picture of him laughing, properly guffawing at something. Perhaps he had just seen Alain Prost trip over his shoelaces. Nevertheless, it seems a somewhat rare spectacle.

Senna did have a sense of fun, of course. He just considered it imperative to keep a professional head on his shoulders during a race weekend. Rather, for the most part at least.

There are several pieces of footage of the usually impassive Brazilian indulging in displays of horsing around, typically when Ron Dennis or his teammate and great friend Gerhard Berger were present. Upon the occasion of his 100th race in 1990, his McLaren team made him a cake which he was obliged to cut in front of the usual army of photographers and journalists. As he helped himself to a slice, very carefully and straight-faced, he suddenly darted forward and dumped it on to the bald head of McLaren team coordinator Jo Ramirez, who happened to be in the wrong place at the wrong time.

There is also footage of him throwing water at both Thierry Boutsen and Berger during photocalls during 1993. There are the numerous stories of him clowning about with the Austrian, the man who proclaims he taught Senna 'how to laugh'. The stories vary depending on from where one hears them, but the gist remains the same.

On one helicopter journey Berger grew tired of Senna's boasts about the robustness of his new briefcase's carbon-fibre construction and threw it out the window to test its owner's claims, and on another occasion replaced Senna's passport photo with a picture of the genitalia of a rather well-endowed gentleman; in retaliation Senna glued Berger's credit cards together.

At the Australian Grand Prix one year, Berger released some amphibious intruders into Senna's hotel room.

'Actually they weren't frogs, they were bigger, more like toads,' he remembers. 'In Australia they have this kind of stuff. I thought he liked animals but clearly not.'

Senna collared the Austrian, fuming 'Do you know I've spent the past hour catching frogs in my room?'

Berger's show-stopping punchline: 'Did you find the snake?'

In his book *Na Reta de Chegada* for the Portuguese market, Berger recalls another encounter.

> After dinner, we started to throw people in the swimming pool, all dressed. As I was good at defending myself, I escaped from the bath, but many people got wet. Senna ran away to avoid us from getting him, however, later, I went to his room and he awkwardly threw a glass of water at me. For a Tyrolean, that was nothing, but it did mean that the game was now on. With a hose, we improvised an extension to the fire extinguisher and we put it under his room door at three in the morning. We invited some people to watch and when we pushed the lever, Senna flew out of the window like a rocket. It looked like a bomb had exploded inside the room. The confusion woke many people up, who started to scream at Senna for making so much noise. He was terribly embarrassed.

Occasionally a third party was involved in the mischief: another Brazilian, Mauricio Gugelmin, who as punishment for filling Berger's shoes with shaving foam before an awards dinner was almost tricked by his victim into drinking sleeping-pill spiked orange juice ten minutes before the start of a Grand Prix.

Gugelmin was a great friend of Senna's, having lived with him in their early days in England, first in Norfolk and then in Esher in Surrey, a house to which they welcomed Mike Doodson: 'All he wanted to do was to get out on to the cricket pitch with his radio controlled models. I took some pictures of that. That was a really nice morning we spent together.'

The humour between the two was evident from a time when neither of them had yet reached Formula 1.

In Tom Rubython's *The Life of Senna*, Dick Bennetts, the man whose West Surrey Racing team took both drivers to British F3 championship glory in 1983 and 1985 respectively, recalls the banter Senna and Gugelmin exchanged, with Senna once giving his younger compatriot the delightfully creative put-down, 'You're so tight you could swim across the Thames with an Alka-Seltzer in your hand and it wouldn't melt.'

I asked Thierry Boutsen for his memories of the lighter side of life with Senna. 'We had lots of funny moments during the moments we spent together, on track and privately in Angra, Portugal, Mauritius. He was a very funny person, great sense of humour,' although he does add, 'but only when time permitted. Everything was super-controlled, no *laisser-aller*!'

Keith Sutton believes Senna, like many of his fellow racers, changed his public face over time as a matter of necessity.

> When I knew him, his sense of humour was good. We're back in those days when I was travelling with him, sharing rooms with him, eating with him, talking about music and girls. You felt as though, in some small way that you had something in common.
>
> I've seen it time and time again with the young drivers coming up through the ranks. They are different people. It all changes when they go to F1 because the world's media is there and even just from GP2 to F1 these days is so, so different – the attention they get, the TV coverage, the money that they earn, the top drivers. It changes them. With that, they've got to be able to focus on driving the car. They've got a lot of sponsor requirements and press requirements.

Witness the number of times Martin Brundle receives a palm in the face on the starting grids of today when he tries to ask them what they hope to achieve at the first corner. He probably wouldn't have appreciated his future self doing the same to him in the years before he became a pundit.

In the modern age, Kimi Raikkonen's bored monotone has been the focus for derision since the moment he first sat in his Sauber in 2001.

Even his rivals joke about it, as Sebastian Vettel demonstrated with his turn as a comedy impressionist at the 2011 *Autosport* awards. And yet it is well known that this is merely the face he presents to the media in his guise of 'Grand Prix driver'. Apparently you can't shut him up when he's out for dinner. When Raikkonen appeared on *Top Gear* in 2012 he was polite, charming and funny. And most people have seen the video of him toppling off the top of a yacht, clearly several Stolichnayas into the afternoon.

Fernando Alonso is the same. Never anything other than focused, determined and eloquent, his personal life remains largely a mystery. When news of his divorce seeped out recently, one could have been forgiven for not realising he was married in the first place.

Lewis Hamilton, on the other hand, *is* a celebrity in every sense of the word and the tabloids can't get enough of him. He is constantly snapped leaving nightclubs, relaxing on beaches and posing for interminable sponsor adverts wearing giant watches or pretending he's excited about cash ISAs. Jenson Button was the same when he first arrived on the scene. This reduces them from being sporting legends to celebrities in fast cars: somehow there is no mystique.

The reason for this dichotomy in Senna's case is that he was smart enough to be nothing other than totally professional when he was in front of the world's TV media. We can only go on anecdotal evidence of what he was like in his down-time – indeed he told Keith Sutton some eye-opening stories that Sutton has vowed never to repeat.

'He had to push a lot of people away. A lot of people that helped him along the way – not just me – all the people he drove for, mechanics, team managers. When he was at the circuit, all he wanted to do was speak to his boss, Ron Dennis, Peter Warr, whoever, and his engineer. That was it really. That is what he was there to do.

'I always found him very pleasant away from the track – at an airport, or if I'd seen him in a restaurant one evening, he was quite normal. Away from the track he had time for people. If you talked to everyone that you knew at an F1 track, you wouldn't be doing your job.'

If a TV camera followed you around your office all day for nine months and you were regularly hauled into press conferences to talk about the performance of your new laser printer compared to the one you had last year, you'd struggle to inject any colour or enthusiasm into it.

And while Senna was often able to introduce a mysteriously poetic element to some of his interviews, the fact is that he was still seen as a very serious and intense young man. Which, when viewed in light of some of the possibly apocryphal stories about him, seems slightly at odds.

Senna's first F1 boss, Alex Hawkridge of Toleman, remembers the day Senna signed his 1984 contract with them: 'We went for a drink in a pub down the road from our headquarters in Brentford, and suddenly Ayrton became a different character. It was as if he switched off from business mode and became this different man. It was as if he just decided that he was done for the day and could start relaxing. He began telling jokes, and that was how we knew that this steely businessman had taken the rest of the day off.'

A year later Senna was again in jovial form when he had agreed to leave Toleman and join Lotus. On his first visit to the Hethel factory, he arrived in style with the Mercedes 190 2.3–16 he had won at the Nurburgring the previous May, and chief spannerman Bob Dance, used to dealing with prima donna racing drivers, decided that he would see what his new charge was made of. While Senna was inside inspecting his new surroundings, the giggling mechanics jacked up his shiny new car and put a block under the differential.

Tour done, Senna headed back to his steed. Peter Warr remembered that 'Of course it had to be the race driver's exit with lots of revs and lots of first gear. When his foot came off the clutch the wheels turned but the car went nowhere.'

Senna apparently took the joshing with good grace but ensured that he got his revenge: at the first race with the team he made sure that Dance ate a sweet that turned his mouth blue for two days.

Later that year, the FIA invited some of the drivers to commentate on the official season review video, temporarily suspending their policy of having one narrator.

To this end those men that had featured prominently that year were asked to lend their voices to footage of their best races. Alain Prost, Michele Alboreto, Stefan Johansson, Nigel Mansell, Keke Rosberg and Niki Lauda all took part, as did Senna. Senna showed a jovial side in his commentary of that year's Portuguese Grand Prix that seems at odds with the methodical approach he took to winning the race. One notable moment occurs when Mauro Baldi, an early retirement in his Spirit-Hart, leaps over the guard-rail only to slip and end up sprawled on his backside. 'Here's Mauro Baldi having a nice landing,' chuckles Senna.

Even as his career progressed and the pressure on him increased, he still enjoyed a laugh when he could.

'Ayrton had a sense of humour that not everybody saw – silly things. On the way to the drivers' briefing [at Monaco] in 1989 he pinched my bum', says Johnny Herbert.

So it seems Senna wasn't humourless at all. He just happened to be rather too good a driver to spend his time messing about.

4

Senna the Driver

Speed and Style

'Prost was much better as a test driver, as an engineer, than Ayrton. For me, Prost was brilliant in a car that suited him, Ayrton was the better driver if they both had bad cars. Ayrton could adapt to any car he had.' says Jo Ramirez.

Senna's driving style arguably developed and matured as his career progressed. Compare and contrast the 1989 and 1993 seasons: in both he was the star of the show but lost the title to Alain Prost. In 1989 he drove with a furious intensity that made you wonder if he asked the McLaren mechanics to nail the throttle to the floor, something that perfectly illustrated the difference between his driving style and that of the Frenchman. Watch an excerpt of the start of every race that year and Senna is always the man on the move. Even if Prost, Berger or Mansell manages to sneak ahead of him, he's all over their gearbox by the first corner and past them again by the second. You can almost see the smoke coming out of his nostrils.

He had a very distinctive way of applying the throttle in the corners – 'applying' being a delicate way of putting it. He would repeatedly stamp on the accelerator in a manner few others did. This was apparently honed from the first five years of his F1 career, in which he drove cars with turbocharged engines: this style would have minimised turbo lag. And of course he spent the first eight seasons of his career changing his own gears. They all did it, of course, but he did it very, very well. A promotional video shot by Honda in the early 1990s follows Senna as he hammers an NSX supercar round Suzuka, with one camera stationed in the footwell to capture him demonstrating the long–lost–to–F1 art of 'heel and toe'. This was when a driver used his right foot to both brake and blip the throttle between downchanges at the same time. His left foot, of course, was busy with the clutch pedal. They really *drove* the car then, and Senna exemplified the driver's artistry.

This robustness with the loud pedal gave him something of a reputation as a tyre–shredding car–breaker, and, compared to Prost, he was, having many more prominent accidents and spins than his French nemesis: that is undeniable. Indeed, Prost went through the entirety of the 1985 – 1988 seasons without damaging a McLaren monocoque!

But Prost himself disagrees with the notion that Senna was difficult on the equipment, saying: 'In the way he drove, he was much more precise than people suppose.'

Indeed, for every Brazil '91 there was an Estoril '91, in which Senna knew he was lucky to cruise to the finish to collect something rather can risk ruining his car and sacrificing championship points. Here's a quote from him at the 1986 Belgian Grand Prix, in which the regulations of the time put a premium on fuel economy: 'I was worried about fuel. Therefore I decided to have six points rather than risk having nothing.'

His tactical approach to winning the 1991 championship in an inferior car belied this maturity. Although he had once said 'I am not designed to come second or third', his Formula 3 team boss Dick Bennetts had to ask him to reconsider his style, and while Senna may have been sincere with this enduring soundbite, he was still happy to collect points on many occasions to ensure he finished first overall.

This was part of the Senna myth that grabbed the public imagination. Prost preferred the Fangio approach, winning as slowly as possible: 'I want to drive all the time if I can at ninety-five per cent. Maybe for one lap I will use ninety-nine per cent. Ayrton went maybe too far in the way he was thinking and driving and competing.'

Where Senna was indisputably the master was in qualifying, when the cars run at as close to their maximum performance as possible. In those days the lap that claimed pole position, set with sticky tyre compounds, maximum turbo boost and mere gasps of fuel, would often be in the region of four seconds faster than the quickest of the race the following day. In Senna's ten and a smidge years in F1 he entered 141 Grands Prix and qualified in top spot 65 times: a conversion rate of 46%. Even when his car was miles off the pace of the best machines he would sneak in an occasional pole or front-row start and surprise everybody. In his peak years there would only be a couple of races in the season where the man with the yellow headgear was not at the front after Saturday lunchtime.

Martin Brundle often fondly reminisces about the snow-plough effect Senna had on the other drivers during practice: 'All the time you'd be looking in your mirrors for the McLaren with the Dayglo helmet.'

A famous clip from Senna's in-car camera during the Spanish Grand Prix in 1989 shows him being baulked by a backmarker, Philippe Alliot, and firing an imaginary pistol at him with his hand from over his windscreen, supporting Brundle's assertions. God help the driver that held Senna up.

Gerhard Berger was no slouch in qualifying himself and earned the distinction of outpacing Senna in their first race together as teammates. But he knew what he was up against. 'You would go quicker and quicker, and finally do a lap – set a time – that you knew was as quick as that car could do. Ayrton, no. He wouldn't accept it. In that situation, he'd somehow generate a power from within himself – he'd find another two or three tenths, and it didn't come from the car ...'

Then there was Senna and the rain …

Many of the great drivers are peerless in the wet, where their superiority in displaying finesse, mechanical sympathy and car control is often enhanced far beyond what is apparent in the dry. Of all the greatest drivers in history, perhaps only Alain Prost has the dubious distinction of either not liking driving in the rain or being unwilling to make the requisite sacrifices. Elsewhere, from Caracciola to Nuvolari, through to Clark and Stewart and Senna and Schumacher, the ability to nurse a Grand Prix car to victory in such totally unsuitable conditions is the mark of someone very special. The most ironic part is how easy they make it look.

History has given us wet races that will never be forgotten: the 1963 Belgian Grand Prix, where Jim Clark finished five minutes ahead of anyone else at the original, white-knuckle Spa circuit and the 1968 German Grand Prix at the equally terrifying Nurburgring that saw fellow Scot Jackie Stewart come in so far ahead of the opposition that he was virtually eating his dinner by the time the rest arrived.

It is often informally said that Finnish drivers make such good rally drivers because of the conditions with which they have to contend in their homeland and the long, dark winter months. Ayrton Senna, brought up with the abundant rainfall of Sao Paulo, had ample opportunities to hone what was not apparently an entirely intuitive talent.

His sister Viviane, the mother of current driver Bruno, remembers in one of his early kart races, Senna floundered in the wet, unable to understand how to approach driving in such low-grip conditions. Thereafter, she says, he would wait like a coiled spring until the skies darkened and, as the first drops began to fall, disappeared to the garage to fire up his kart. While others may have pulled on their pac-a-mac, Senna donned his crash helmet and headed out into the deluge. He did this repeatedly until he had mastered the conditions. It obviously worked. Senna didn't want for talent, but any gaps that were there at this early stage of his career were soon filled by the fierce determination that is the preserve of all world-class sportsmen.

Senna lifted many victories when the conditions were appalling, most famously his first win at Estoril in 1985 and one of his last when he trounced the Williams duo of Prost and Hill at Donington in 1993. The Donington race demonstrated his intuitive knowledge of how much grip a corner would offer him before he even arrived. He didn't always get it right, as evidenced at the 1989 Canadian and Australian Grands Prix and the Spanish Grand Prix of 1991, but then again, nobody's perfect, as Senna himself once acknowledged.

Charisma and determination

Suddenly I realised that I was no longer driving the car consciously. I was kind of driving by instinct, only I was in a different dimension. I was way over the limit, but still I was able to find even more. It frightened me because I realised I was well beyond my conscious understanding.

Speaking after his famous Monaco pole lap of 1988, Senna served to reinforce the perpetuating consensus is that he was more than just a Grand Prix driver; he was, instead, an illusionist or a magician.

People often remark on Formula 1 racers 'doing their talking on the track', a polite way of saying they are boring interviewees. But Senna did his talking everywhere!

Compared to Alain Prost's quiet, technically-minded answers (which, it has to be said, were more often than not making excuses) and Nigel Mansell's monotonous foghorn drawl, Senna's passionate delivery in interviews was mesmerising. He did not possess a booming baritone voice, but it was often loud and clear. He also looked directly at the person to whom he was speaking, as opposed to his shoes.

When Prost was telling the press that his race was stymied by a broken oil temperature read-out, it was as dull as it sounded. Senna, meanwhile, could sound like he was reading poetry even if he was merely talking about tyre valve caps. He was a superb orator. The Muhammad Ali of Formula 1. 'Brevity' was not in his vocabulary, although he was always painstakingly meticulous when answering a question, sometimes pausing for large swathes of time before answering, especially in languages other than Portuguese.

He was effortlessly charismatic. He wasn't necessarily the only driver of that era with this quality, but he undoubtedly upped the glamour quotient. Rivals like Nelson Piquet and Keke Rosberg were also a pressman's dream, but Senna was the whole package.

Although when Senna was in Brazil it often seemed he would rather stick his finger in a pencil sharpener than return to pound round the test tracks, when he was at the circuit his devotion was second to none. He and Alain Prost would spend hours in technical briefings, neither wanting to betray a weakness or concede an advantage by leaving early.

Contemporaries gave F1 everything they could, but that isn't the same as *everything*. Other Grand Prix drivers had other distractions outside the F1 world. David Coulthard, who worked as a test driver at Williams with both Senna and Nigel Mansell, drew attention to this when talking about a session in early 1994:

'After the second day, Senna had a small incident and tweaked his neck and that was it, test over. I came in the following day and he was there. I thought, "Okay, he must have had a miraculous recovery", but in actual fact he was just there to listen to what I said to the engineers. Whereas Nigel Mansell would set a time and bugger off to the golf course.'

Even when Senna did allow himself a bit of downtime, he still couldn't stay away from things with engines: either blasting around with his nephew and niece on his jetski or taking to the nearest open space with his model aeroplane. In his later years, he did start to expand his interests with his business portfolio but, by and large, he had 'F1 driver' written through him like a stick of rock.

Senna had no children, not that he knew about anyway. It is possible that he was able to find that extra dimension, motivation, compared to contemporaries like Prost, Mansell and Berger who all had families of their own. That freedom undoubtedly gives a driver something of an edge, whether he realises it or not. When Fernando Alonso overtook Michael Schumacher around the outside of Suzuka's 130R corner in the supremely entertaining Japanese Grand Prix of 2005, he explained why he thought the audacious move would stick. 'At times like that I always remember Michael has two children.'

Independence and Belligerence

Senna was, in the words of Derek Warwick, 'one of the greatest drivers of all time, but the loneliest man in Formula 1'.

It isn't hard to see why. By all accounts, once one was inside Senna's circle he was a generous, kind and funny man. But he was also incredibly picky about who was allowed in and who wasn't, and fellow Grand Prix drivers had to fight damn hard if they wanted to be granted entrance.

Martin Whitmarsh, who worked with him at McLaren says, 'I don't know anyone who knew Ayrton. Ayrton, I believe, was an absolute competitor and he was absolutely private. I hear people say that they were his good friends, but I don't remember so many people being around him. I don't know that many people knew the real Ayrton Senna.'

Thierry Boutsen was a rare exception. 'We were friends. Real friends. And friends discuss lots of things, feelings, decisions. Friends try to help each other. It goes without saying that we did not always agree on everything, but each cared about the other. My view is that Ayrton was always fair but hard with the other drivers. His desire to win was stronger than any other driver. Like in all top sports, the hard way is the only way!'

This all makes sense, of course. Senna, for whatever reason, had a 'me against the world' mentality, strange for a man who enjoyed such a privileged upbringing, and seemed to genuinely believe that he couldn't rise to the top without leaving people lying mangled by the roadside in his wake. You can see where he was coming from, even if it is questionable whether such belligerence was always necessary. An early photo of Senna shows him holding Formula Ford rival Enrique Mansilla round the throat while staring into his eyes. It is safe to assume that he wasn't congratulating him.

Another of Senna's old Formula Ford 2000 nemeses, Calvin Fish, said of him: 'He personally felt he was head and shoulders above everyone else ...when it came to [being beaten] he didn't know how to handle it.' And this an opinion formed in 1982.

Even Murray Walker, known for keeping his opinions largely to himself, said 'I always thought that he was just too intense about winning, and actually believed he had a God-given right to win.'

By the time he was a world champion, Senna had a collection of figures for whom he reserved his greatest professional distaste. These included Nelson Piquet (with good reason, as we shall discover later), Nigel Mansell and later Michael Schumacher. But the two for whom he reserved the greatest revulsion were the late Jean-Marie Balestre and Alain Prost.

Senna and Balestre never saw eye-to-eye, and only in part because Balestre continually insisted on wearing sunglasses. His past was equally shady and he had alleged links to some rather suspect characters in his youth, according to his 2008 obituary in *The Guardian*, once taking legal action to stifle photographs of him wearing a German SS uniform. This reflected much of his character. He rubbed many F1 figures up the wrong way in his tenure as the head of FISA, the sport's governing body, and Senna was no exception. His autocratic leadership style was memorably encapsulated in the driver's briefing for the 1991 German Grand Prix when he insisted, 'the best decision is my decision'. Balestre's treatment of Senna in the witch-hunt of 1989 was after all as subtle as opening a beer can with a bulldozer.

On the other hand, Alain Prost did not altogether deserve the treatment he received at the hands of his Brazilian counterpart. Prost was no media darling himself, and he was a shrewd and quietly political operator who seemed to have a deleterious effect on team principals for whom he worked. But in Senna's eyes, his crime was to be the best.

When Senna knew he would be joining McLaren in 1988, then very much Prost's team, he told the outfit's former driver John Watson that he didn't just want to beat Prost, he wanted to annihilate him in every way. And in later seasons he was almost as good as his word. It is curious that Prost was Senna's most loathed rival in one way – with a single noteworthy exception, he never bullied him, drove into him, withheld information from him or undermined him. Other drivers used to tangle with Senna every other weekend, and yet Prost was the one whose face adorned Senna's dartboard. The punishment hardly fitted the crime.

'Ayrton was different, nobody really understands this,' says Prost. 'You can say all good things about him, but you cannot compare him to a normal racing driver. Never. You do not realize that immediately.'

And yet, it is doubtful whether Senna truly hated Prost, in the truest sense of the word. His sister Viviane says he told her 'life is too short for enemies'. Prost himself says the two of them had 'a strange kind of friendship, hidden by the fights we had'.

That Senna respected Prost cannot be in doubt. He said it himself: 'You may find it funny, because I have lots of criticism from those mentioned, [but] I admire a lot Prost by his results, Mansell by his determination and his results too. We have differences in many areas but that doesn't change the fact that they have achieved great results and great situations which you've got to admire, got to respect.'

John Hogan was the main man at McLaren title sponsor Marlboro for many years. He knew both drivers well and describes Ayrton thus: 'I don't think he was shy. I think he was emotionally immature throughout his whole career. He was a bit of a spoiled baby at home. Every thinking second was consumed with his desire to win.'

Contemporary Honda PR officer Eric Silbermann says: 'Prost wasn't exactly a laugh a minute – but neither was Senna. Senna was a nice bloke, and I always got a Christmas card that was personally signed and specific to me. But he could be a complete prick to work with at times.'

One hypothesis is that Senna only disliked people on a professional level, and when that threat to his dominance was gone, he saw no reason to continue with hostilities.

When Balestre lost the presidency of the FIA to Max Mosley in 1991, he would no longer be a nuisance to Senna. The Brazilian had made it known in very strident terms what he thought of his tormentor, but with the finish of the 1991 season he presumably thought enough was enough. While he had to be pressed to reveal details, he admitted that at the end of that year he had given Balestre a gift to bury the hatchet: a crash helmet of his which he was able to give 'sincerely'.

He said: 'We made some jokes and I was able to express some of my feelings in a sincere manner but at the same time without any knife anywhere, really sincere and joking. It just came right and I believe he took it in the right way. I think it was good. It happened unexpectedly but I was happy afterwards that it happened in that way.'

Two years later, when Prost called time on his great career, he suggested a similar reconciliatory gesture in front of the press corps in Japan.

As we walked from the podium to the press conference, I said to him, 'This may be the last race where we are at a press conference together, and I think we should show the people something nice – maybe shake hands, or something.' He didn't answer me, but he didn't say no, either, so I thought maybe he agreed. We went to the press conference – and he wouldn't even look at me.

In fact, I'd even thought maybe in Australia [the next race, two weeks later] we could exchange helmets, the last helmets we'd worn in a race against each other – but after Japan, I forgot about it, because he hadn't seemed interested in any sort of reconciliation.

Come their final race together in Australia two weeks later, Senna won and Prost was indeed alongside him in second. Senna pulled Prost up on to the top step of the podium to stand alongside him.

Prost was gobsmacked: 'From this moment where I am on the podium, close to him, on the same level, he changed completely. He was really another person. You had [Ayrton] before this podium and after this podium. It was absolutely unbelievable. It was a different person, a different driver, different personality in my opinion. At the press conference, he was speaking and asking questions to me as he has never talked before.'

Prost was no mug and he knew that this was all being done on Senna's terms, but it didn't make him any less astounded.

Nonetheless, there were still new figures coming up through the ranks able to take the place of Senna's past irritants.

After his amazing début in 1991, Michael Schumacher was behind the wheel of the Benetton-Ford from his second Grand Prix onward. He announced himself as a new star with a win at Spa in his first full season the next year, making it clear that he feared no one: 'I am not the new Ayrton Senna: I am Michael Schumacher.'

In Brazil that year he felt that Senna was messing him about by lifting slightly on the straights, and broadcast his displeasure at the incident to the media: 'Ayrton was quite slow. I was quicker than him all the time, but I had no chance to pass him, and after ten laps or so he start to play a game. He knew he couldn't finish so he just brake in the slow corners and on the straight he just go on the throttle back and drove away from us ... I'm very upset about this. I think it is not really necessary for a three-times world champion to do something like this.'

This didn't go down at all well with the elder statesman, nor was it forgotten. At the French Grand Prix in July, Schumacher ran him off at the Adelaide hairpin and Senna would take no further part when the race restarted. In the lull between the first and second parts of the Grand Prix Senna, dressed in sweater and jeans (no sponsor-adorned team casualwear then) approached Schumacher for a word.

An audacious (or intrusive, depending on your viewpoint) reporter stuck a microphone between them but Senna irritably pushed it away as one might a yappy dog. What they did manage to capture was Senna accusing the German of 'giving me sh*t.' Senna told the German to speak to him rather than whinge to the press if he had a problem with him.

'If you f*ck it [a race] up, I come and talk to you,' he scolded, keeping a persuasive grip on Schumacher's shoulder. The pair later clashed in testing at Hockenheim, with Senna feeling aggrieved enough by the younger man's actions to grab him round the collar in the Benetton garage, an incident captured by a photographer's lens and brushed off by Schumacher as nothing more than a 'little massage'.

Come 1993, Senna was starting to feel the heat from the new generation of drivers.

Before the Portuguese Grand Prix McLaren showed his American teammate Michael Andretti the door and promoted their test driver Mika Hakkinen, who rattled Senna's cage by outqualifying him first time out. Senna shouted at Hakkinen, 'How many pole positions have you had? How many?' but the Finn remained unfazed.

'He wasn't very happy', Hakkinen remembers in his classically understated way.

In Japan the next time out, Hakkinen was once again close to Senna's practice times and followed his teammate on to the podium in the race. David Tremayne's post-qualifying piece for *The Independent,* entitled 'Ascent of Hakkinen Unsettles Senna' opened with 'The old order is beginning to change at last …'

Hakkinen was not the only young charger giving Senna problems at Suzuka.

Ulsterman Eddie Irvine, a graduate from the Formula Nippon series in Japan, was making his Grand Prix début for the Jordan team, for whom he had driven in Formula 3000, replacing a stream of disappointing partners for Rubens Barrichello that year. He qualified eighth and rocketed up to fifth at the start, overtaking future teammate Michael Schumacher around the outside of the S curves and holding his own against faster machinery.

Later in the race, when Senna was en route to victory and had already lapped Irvine, the Jordan driver famously re-passed the McLaren after cheekily proclaiming that Senna was 'too slow'.

After the victory celebrations, during which some said Gerhard Berger was doing an excellent job of both winding up his friend and plying him with drink, Senna stormed into the Jordan garage to look for the transgressor, giving the Jordan driver a verbal bashing within earshot of F1 journalist Adam Cooper, who was recording the whole thing. After a bad-tempered exchange of words, during which he called Irvine a 'f*cking idiot', Senna made to leave but then turned and punched him, shouting 'You got to learn to respect where you're going wrong!'

Undoubtedly Irvine's actions were both ill-advised and irritating, but Senna's aggression was seen by many as unfounded, especially considering he had won the race easily. It wasn't exactly the most Christian behaviour. Senna was given a suspended ban for his trouble.

Irvine was an open admirer of Senna in his youth, even using the same helmet design in his early days, but he was less enamoured with the Brazilian after this incident.

But none of this should be a surprise. Senna was sometimes an unrepentantly ruthless man.

He was guilty of introducing a portfolio of over-aggressive tactics to the top tier of motorsport, through which other drivers have undoubtedly riffled on several occasions since.

Richard Williams, author of the fascinating *The Death of Ayrton Senna,* says: 'He really was a pure product of kart racing and he brought to F1 a way of racing that until that time had been particular to karts which was a very no-compromise kind of approach. Physical contact between the machines was OK, was safe enough. But to bring that into cars was something quite different. And that was one of things that shocked his slightly older rivals. The etiquette that they grew up with was different, was rooted in the belief that you didn't make contact with another rival's car because if you did that you were likely to die.'

Therefore, it seems peculiar Senna has been granted a hagiographic status despite being, at times, arguably one of the more dangerous competitors the sport has seen. Perhaps it was all part of what his last girlfriend Adriane Galisteu referred to when she said that away from the track her partner was Ayrton, but as soon as he donned the overalls and famous yellow helmet he became 'Senna'. In that moment, the introspective, spiritual man who would spend flights on his private jet immersed in his Bible would become the figure out of whose way all but the most fearless drivers would leap. As he himself said: 'The helmet hides feelings that cannot be understood.'

Nigel Roebuck, whose entertaining race reports for *Autosport* magazine covered the entirety of Senna's career, once wrote: 'He was such a strange man. Kind, fundamentally, even gentle, yet capable – in extremis – of actions that bordered on madness. If ever a racing driver were incapable of compromise, it was Ayrton Senna,' adding, perhaps controversially, 'and of course that's what killed him.'

Senna's behaviour occasionally suggested that his emotions were undergoing a dichotomous tug-of-war, between a concern for his fellow man and a desire to prove himself better than everyone else at all costs. For every piece of questionable manoeuvring on track, Senna exhibited as many if not more displays of courage and altruism towards his fellow drivers, as we have touched on.

Brundle says, 'He'd be the first man to run you off the road and then the first man to run back and see if you were okay.'

'Ayrton was an exceptional person, very kind, generous, open to the people close to him,' says Thierry Boutsen. 'But he was also a racer, very determined to win, 100% focused. His skills added to that made of him the best racing driver of his time. Although he respected the other drivers competing against him, he hated them [only] as much as they hated him. Trying to be friends with an athlete [against whom you are competing] is for losers.'

Keith Sutton agrees: 'It's very difficult to have friends if you're a racing driver: you're competing against them.'

Senna didn't just like to win on the track either. He wanted to win at everything he put his hand to, as do many extremely competitive individuals. Early in his career, he was offered a deal with Arai helmets but chose to delay for as long as possible to try and squeeze as much as possible out of the Japanese company. He left it too late and, when it seemed he had missed his chance, he panicked and tried to re-open negotiations. The reply? 'Dear Mr Senna, I'm afraid we don't have a helmet big enough for your head.'

Even when he was shopping, the Brazilian struck fear into the hearts of market traders and business owners alike, beating vendors down on price for the sheer enjoyment of doing it rather than because he intended to buy anything.

As we will see later, Senna had his fair share of contractual quibbles for most of his Grand Prix career, but his dealings with Ron Dennis have become the most well known.

While Dennis probably wouldn't have been able to win at Monaco on six occasions, when it came to financial negotiations he found himself to be much a much more equal adversary for his Brazilian employee. He has often told the famous story of the coin–flipping incident but it was not the only occasion he found himself eyeballing Senna across a negotiating table.

Mike Doodson remembers another famous encounter: 'In Mexico [before the Grand Prix of 1989], Ron was having dinner with Senna. There was a bowl of chillies in the middle of the table, and Ron tried one and said "Crikey, they're hot" and I believe it was Senna who said "I'll give you a thousand dollars if you eat the lot of them". The two were so driven and competitive that Ron took him on, as he thought all he had to was swallow them. But what Ron had forgotten was what would happen to him the next morning, which Senna probably knew!'

Senna was well known for giving no quarter in negotiations and Dennis knew this about him from early on:

> The first time I met him, he was in Formula Ford going into F3. I offered to pay for his F3 championship in return for an option on his services. I cannot remember the words, but he was very clear in telling me that he would pay for his own F3 season. He did not want anything but a guarantee of a drive instead of an option. And this was a young guy who had not really proven himself but had the self-belief that he was going to be a tremendous F1 driver.

> That was the first encounter and when we parted I thought, 'arrogant young Brazilian'.

It wasn't the last time that Senna and Dennis would have a difference of opinion over contractual issues. By the time the pair were in their last season together in 1993 their competitive nature meant that the relationship had gone off-colour.

Senna knew he was saddled with an inferior car and wished to remind Dennis of what he thought he was worth. He didn't need a million dollars per Grand Prix, but he asked and got it anyway. Dennis admitted to *Autosport* many years later that this gargantuan sum compromised McLaren's research and development efforts. It was even more notable given that Senna had reputedly told Frank Williams that he would drive his car for free. It must be said that if he was really that keen to divert funds from his own account to make sure that he had the best car possible, he had a funny way of showing it.

At the San Marino Grand Prix that year Senna only just arrived on time, on the back of a scooter. His private pilot Captain O'Mahony wasn't even to bother leafing through his pre-flight checks if Ron Dennis hadn't deposited the million dollars in his employer's bank account, and Senna was staying put in Brazil until the last minute.

The normally affable Jo Ramirez lost his rag with Senna, when he eventually arrived, for making the McLaren team run around like 'headless chickens' after him. Senna promptly drove like one, crashing in practice and then retiring from the damp race. This may have led to Dennis allegedly calling him 'unemployable'.

Hypocrisy

The clearest example of this aspect of the Brazilian's character is illustrated by the circumstances leading to the selection of potential teammates for both 1986 and 1993.

In 1986, Senna had only two years of F1 behind him and found himself at the good but not-quite-good-enough Lotus team. His 1985 teammate Elio de Angelis had exited stage left, unable to cope with the way Senna had rallied the team around him.

This left a space in the number 11 car and John Player Special, the British-owned cigarette brand whose black and gold colours had provided Lotus's iconic liveries from 1972, wanted a British driver: Derek Warwick.

When the shortlist got through to Senna, he unhesitatingly put a red pen through Derek's name. The team was forced to plump for Johnny Dumfries, a landed gent with a full name so long it would have necessitated a limousine spec Lotus to have fitted it all on to the engine cover. He was actually a decent driver: he had won the British F3 Championship the year after his new teammate, but he hadn't a prayer. He put in some solid showings, but with little time to acclimatise to the Lotus environment, he was permanently on the back foot. Said Warwick:

> You have to admire [Senna] for sticking to what he thought was right ... He was hated by a lot of fans and a lot of the press, but he stuck to his guns. I would not have done that to another human being but that's probably why I'm not a great champion. No matter how you analyse it now – and I bear Senna no malice whatsoever – he destroyed my career as a top Grand Prix driver. Even now, my wife Rhonda won't hear of his name in the house.

Not everyone is wholly in opposition to Senna's behaviour toward Warwick, however.

'I totally disagree with the received opinion on vetoing Derek Warwick,' contends Mike Doodson:

> Lotus only had a very limited budget. Senna knew that there were not going to be able to produce two race-

winning cars that year, so he vetoed Warwick because he knew that Derek, as a British driver, would be favoured by John Player, who were putting in quite a lot of money but not enough to run two equal cars. If you do the analysis of that year when Johnny Dumfries drove for them, you'll find that they had only one example of the new gearbox. Johnny had to run the old one, which was very weak, which broke in God knows how many races …go through the results of the 1986 season and you'll see that Dumfries retired with transmission failure in a large number of races.

Senna knew in advance that it was going to be the same for whoever was his number two. He was aware of the fact that if the driver was Derek Warwick, JPS would have wanted to favour Warwick and it would have split the efforts of the team and detracted from his own season. He had the right under his contract to be consulted on the second driver and I think that his judgment was correct, because it meant that at least one of the Lotuses that year would be competitive.

Warwick would only return to F1, ironically, as a replacement for de Angelis at the Brabham team after the Italian's death. Whilst Senna probably would not have been welcome at any Warwick family soirees after this fracas, even Derek admits that at least Senna had the balls to approach him and apologise.

As Doodson succinctly puts it: 'Formula 1 is a hard business. It's not a ladies' embroidery class.'

This is the work of a hard-nosed b*****d perhaps, but is it hypocrisy? John Hogan again:

'Alain Prost was very much of the view that you have to beat the best somehow, so he had no problem that Ayrton was in the same team. Ayrton did not hold that view. He stopped anyone that was good from getting in the other car. He whinged like f*ck.'

The man certainly shoots from the hip. He is right though, and here's why:

Many years after the Warwick controversy in 1992, Senna was a triple world champion and yet pedalling a McLaren that would have struggled to a pole position, let alone a world title. He desperately wanted to get himself back into the best car, which at the time was the Williams-Renault. But his old pal Prost had stolen a march on him by signing for them already. Not only that, the Frenchman had told Frank that whoever was in the second seat alongside him, his first name was not to be Ayrton and his second name was not to be Senna.

The public got wind of this during the 1992 Portuguese Grand Prix weekend. When asked about his views on the topic, Senna had this to say:

'One thing I will say is that it's supposed to be a world driver's championship. I think if Prost wants to be called a three times world champion, come back in a sportive way and maybe win another championship, he should be sportive. The way he's doing, he is behaving like a coward. If he wants to be sportive, he must be prepared to race anybody, at any condition, in equal terms, and not the way he wants to win the championship.

'It's like if you go in a 100m sprint, and you want to have running shoes, and everybody else should have lead shoes. That's the way he wants to race. This is not racing and it's bad to all of us. That's it.'

It was, on one hand, arguably the action of a spoiled child who was raging that he had been outfoxed. Not only did it make him seem highly hypocritical in light of what he had done to Derek Warwick in 1986, he would have done well to remember that it was his own aggressive attitude towards Prost, who hitherto had had no problems with any of his McLaren teammates (two of whom were world champions), that prompted the Frenchman to veto him.

But, as Doodson says, 'The words "hypocritical" and "Senna" fit reasonably comfortably into the same sentence.'

Part Two

5

In the Beginning

As a racing driver Ayrton Senna first came to the wider world's attention in 1984, but his career in single-seaters had started three years earlier and his life in professional karts as early as 1973.

Back then he was simple Ayrton da Silva, until in 1983 he decided to begin using his mother's maiden name instead of his rather commonplace surname, figuring 'Senna' had more allure. He wasn't wrong.

Damon Hill admits that British drivers like himself just weren't able to command the same levels of mysticism. The names 'Nigel Mansell', 'Derek Warwick' and 'Martin Brundle' bring to mind pork butchers or the proprietors of hardware stores. 'Nelson Piquet' and 'Ayrton Senna' somehow do not.

Brazil was already a successful exporter of racing drivers, having already seen two of their compatriots crowned Formula 1 world champion before Ayrton Senna arrived on the scene.

Emerson Fittipaldi was one of Senna's boyhood idols and a fellow Paulista. A conscientious and intelligent individual, with a fearsome pair of sideburns to boot, he had won only his fifth Grand Prix after being drafted in to replace the late Jochen Rindt at Lotus. Two years after his début win at Watkins Glen in 1970, Fittipaldi would be crowned the youngest ever world champion at the age of 25, a record that would stand until Fernando Alonso's triumphant year in 2005.

He was champion again for McLaren in 1974, after one of the closest seasons in the sport's history. After a further season with the British team in 1975, he made the decision to join his brother Wilson's Copersucar team, which would carry the family sur-name in a later incarnation. Emerson was never to win another Formula 1 race, despite employing a recent UCL graduate by the name of Adrian Newey towards the end of his tenure. In each of the five seasons he struggled with uncompetitive machinery and a different driver won the championship, leaving one wondering what more he could have achieved with such open competition. After his departure from F1 in 1980, he took a four-year break before resuming his racing career in the US. This turned out to be a smarter move than his previous career choice and in 1989 he won both the CART title and the Indy 500 at the ripe age of 42.

Rio de Janeiro's Nelson Piquet lifted his first title in 1981 and added two more in 1983 and 1987. Although devastatingly fast on his day, he won his three championships with a mixture of guile and consistency rather than by annihilating the opposition. Ironically, in the one season when he didn't lift the title, 1984, he was on pole position more than anyone else but couldn't translate his front-row starts into wins as his Brabham-BMW was out-classed by the McLaren-TAGs.

His stock was somewhat reduced in value in 1986 and 1987 when he was partnered with Nigel Mansell at Williams and the Briton, definitely the number 2 and whose relative salary would have barely bought him a moustache-trimmer, had the nerve to keep beating him.

Piquet always affected an air of nonchalance and was certainly renowned as one of Grand Prix racing's more colourful charac-ters, but he could have a nasty side as well. This became particu-larly prevalent when he realised the intense young upstart from Sao Paulo had usurped him in the affections of the Brazilian crowd. Unable to get on terms with either Senna or Mansell on track, he famously gave the Brazilian edition of *Playboy* a rather underhand interview in which he accused Senna of harbouring homosexual proclivities and Mansell of being 'an uneducated blockhead with a stupid and ugly wife'. He later admitted that he had nothing against the Englishman at all: he was just trying to undermine him.

Ayrton (pronounced 'Aye-air-ton') Senna da Silva was born on 21 March 1960 in Santana, a suburb of Sao Paulo. His parents Milton and Neide already had a daughter, Viviane, and would have another son, Leonardo.

He initially suffered from such poor hand-to-eye coordination that his parents sought medical attention, but thankfully young Ayrton was not destined to join the ranks of clumsy kids who get laughed at when they miss the ball during class soccer matches, and his interest in motorsport curiously changed his cack-handedness overnight. Viviane remembers her little brother being taken out to buy shoes as a child and replicating the sounds of revving engines and screeching brakes as he charged around the shop. When Milton da Silva piqued his son's enthusiasm by building him a little go-kart using an old lawnmower engine, the transformation was complete.

For added allure Milton bolted the race number '007' to the front of the chassis – 'Ayrton da Silva – License to Win' – although the effect was tainted somewhat by the fact that it was upside down.

While still at school, Senna started racing karts in his homeland and soon adopted the distinctive crash helmet bedecked with the colours of the Brazilian *bandeira* that would later become arguably the most famous helmet design there has ever been. It was created for Senna by Sid Mosca, who had also created helmets for Fittipaldi. Mosca says that although the colours were chosen on a patriotic basis, the main consideration behind the helmet's design was aggression, as the two horizontal lines angled downwards drew attention to Senna's intense eyes, and the bright yellow could be seen a mile off. Modern Grand Prix stars who feel the need to change their colours every time they make a pit stop would do well to take notice.

For his first kart race he was required to draw lots to determine his grid position rather than undergo actual qualifying time
trials. Even so, his career started much as it ended when he drew
pole position out of the hat. His tiny stature enabled him to
outdrag his rivals on the straight even though they were far
superior in the corners, so he stayed ahead. Little Ayrton eventually retired from his début race but the die had been cast.

Surprisingly, despite racing karts at a professional level for ten
seasons, Senna was never crowned world champion, something
he felt remorseful about until the end of his life. He even
continued to try for the championship when he was a Formula
Ford 2000 racer aged 22.

He did, however, win the South American title in 1977 and
was runner-up in the world title running twice. For the man who
once said 'I am not designed to come second or third' it was an
anomaly that he never took the laurels for this most fiercely-
fought of competitions, but he did not forget his love of the
simplest form of motorsport. Even when he was F1 world
champion, he rated his rivalry with Terry Fullerton for the 1980
title as being his toughest, and Fullerton his most worthy adversary. Although, Senna being Senna, this didn't stop him shoving
the Englishman into a swimming pool on one occasion when he
dared to beat him!

While his numerous seasons of karting hadn't quite delivered
the success that he craved, a move to Formula Ford for 1981
married the Brazilian with a medium with which he would have
infinitely more results – the single-seater racing car.

Senna took the difficult decision to move to England, as had
many of his compatriots, so as to be close to the headquarters of
many of the major motorsport organisations.

'I had in my mind a very strong desire to succeed as a
professional, not only as a hobby. And for that, you have to cope
with some difficulties that come around,' he said. 'That meant I
had to learn to live in a different country, away from my own

people. And if that was not [such a] good side of my new lifestyle, on the other hand I was fulfilling – slowly – a personal goal.'

When he first arrived he couldn't cook and derived his nourishment from eggs prepared in various ways – which isn't very many! Any wonder he earned, as his personal trainer Nuno Cobra revealed, the media nickname 'Skinny Ayrton Senna'.

When he wasn't in the kitchen he watched British TV for hours on end in order to learn the unfamilar English language and even did a bit of gardening.

A neighbour in the Reading street on which he later lived, Chelsea Close in Tilehurst, still remember the young man who 'planted all these rose bushes at the front. His gardening skills were pretty bad!'

Ray Hawkins was one of Senna's neighbours at the time, and one day he was horrified when his brother reversed into Senna's little silver Alfasud, which was parked across the street.

'There was no one around and he drove off and left me to sort it out. I put a note through his door and Senna's friend came round and told me not to worry about it. He said Ayrton had plenty of money and to forget about it. He thanked me for letting him know who had done it.'

There is now an Ayrton Senna Road around the corner from where he lived: not quite a fitting tribute somehow, but a pleasant gesture nonetheless.

Before Reading, Senna's first stop in England was Norfolk so he could be near the offices of the Van Diemen Formula Ford team.

Coming from a life of comparative comfort in balmy Sao Paulo, Ayrton initially struggled to adapt to life in England, insisting on having his gloves put over the radiator before races to chase off the chills.

Senna wasn't alone, however. He had married his beautiful girlfriend Liliane in 1981 and brought her with him to keep him company, to the delight of many mechanics up and down British pitlanes. However, motor racing bored Liliane to tears and worried her in equal measure. Whereas Senna at least had his nascent profession to focus on, she had little to do but click stopwatches and drink tea, trailing after her husband and watching interminable rounds of a sport in which she had no interest whatsoever at freezing, rainy race circuits.

Doodson reckons that the move was definitely easier for Senna than Liliane.

> Senna knew how to balance things out at the beginning of his career: he knew he had to spend the winter in this country. He got married to Liliane very early on. He was only 21. It's a sign of his ruthlessness, to my mind, that he obliged her to come and live in a ghastly little semi-detached house in Norfolk through an English winter when she was only 19 years old. That was an early sign of his ruthlessness. He needed some Brazilian company. He persuaded this girl to marry him and keep him company in very unpleasant circumstances.

Keith Sutton met the young Senna (then da Silva) for the first time that year.

> I was in my second year. I was 21, he was 20 so we were more or less the same age. I was doing Formula 2, Formula 3, Formula Ford, and I'd done a couple of Grands Prix, but the big plan was, like any young driver, to get to Formula 1. I was at Thruxton working for a Brazilian motorsport magazine that wanted photographs of Brazilian drivers racing in England. I was shy in those days so I never introduced myself [to Senna] – I just took lots of photographs of him, in the paddock, on the track – he must have wondered why this photographer he had

never seen before was taking so many rolls of film of him at only his second event in a racing car.

Senna had signed to drive for Van Diemen for the 1981 season, competing in two Formula Ford championships – the RAC and Townsend-Thoresen. In his first race at Brands Hatch, he finished fifth, in his second at Thruxton, third.

For the third round of the Townsend-Thoreson championship on March 15, Senna and the field returned to Brands Hatch. This race represented another microcosm of the Senna legend. In true British style it rained, but this didn't deter Senna from finishing first in his qualifying heat and claiming pole position. Come the race, he reeled off 15 laps of Brands' Indy circuit and was never headed, coming home 9.4 seconds ahead of Alfonso Toledano to lift his first victory in emphatic style.

Sutton captured the now-famous series of photos of Senna, grinning broadly (and modeling that decade's must-have accessory: a digital Casio watch with a built-in calculator) as he stands with his beaming wife and his winner's cheque for seventy pounds, about £220 in today's money.

Sutton admits that it took him a while to realise how good Senna was – after all, Fittipaldi and Piquet had paved the way for the South American contingent to come to Britain and they were now ten-a-penny:

When I met him, he was just another driver who wanted pictures and wanted to pay for them, and I hadn't realised how special he was. At that point there were his teammates [Enrique] Mansilla from Argentina and Toledano from Mexico. They seemed to be just as good: the three of them had some good battles together.

After three months or so, when he carried on winning, then he started to build a team around him. He was doing that even in those days. That's when it became apparent that he was pretty special. A lot of the time he wasn't just competing against these young drivers, he was competing against some established Formula Ford racers like Rick Morris who were very good and had been around for years.

Over time the friendship between the two men developed and Senna entrusted Sutton with other aspects of his career: 'I did all his press releases after each race. He never wanted to check them or anything. I did it all and sent them out to all the F1 team principals and magazines around the world. I was definitely one of the first people to do an interview with him, published in *Autosprint* in Italy.'

Senna's season was a huge success and he won at a quite ridiculous rate, inevitably landing both titles by the year's end. Yet incredibly, given the sacrifices that Senna had made for his career, he came very close to packing everything in at the end of 1981 and going home.

The reasons that he gave at the time were myriad, but he was totally honest. He was homesick, he was worried about raising finance for his second season in car racing since the Brazilian economy was in trouble, his family wanted him to knuckle down to a real job and help out with their business interests and, although it was kept quiet, his marriage was in trouble, which given Liliane's ennui from start to finish wasn't a colossal surprise. Over the winter of 1981/82 they went their separate ways.

'If I was going to make it to Formula 1, I had to give it all my time and attention. I couldn't do that if I was married, so we parted.'

Senna was saddened that his marriage had not worked out, but the trademark ruthlessness was still very much in evidence and when he arrived back in England in February to return to what he did best, there was no doubt in his mind as to which had been the right path to take.

Despite his open admission of the reasons behind his sabbatical, others still had their doubts as to what was really behind it.

Dundalk-born Tommy Byrne, as with Terry Fullerton in 1980, was a thorn in Ayrton's side and a genuine threat to his crown as the most talented driver of the era. He, like Senna, was Formula Ford 1600, Formula Ford 2000 and British Formula 3 champion successively, every year preceding the Brazilian's triumphs.

In his autobiography *Crashed and Byrned* (incidentally one of the most entertaining books ever written about motor racing) the Irishman recalls an early and not entirely friendly encounter with Senna.

On one memorable occasion not longer after his return from Brazil Senna burst into the offices of Van Diemen, for whom they were both works driver, and collared Byrne.

'You f*cking thief. You stole my f*cking wheels.'

Byrne had indeed 'borrowed' a couple of the wheels from Senna's Alfasud to use on his own, as the former had been cutting a lonesome figure in the Van Diemen car park while its intended user luxuriated at home in Brazil. It wasn't even Senna's car, merely one that he was using and which Byrne had sourced for him through a contact at Firman's behest. He, apparently, never paid for it!

Mark Hughes, the book's co-author, asks whether Senna was perhaps threatened by the challenge that Byrne posed to him, and wondered if his tactics meant that he would avoid going up against Byrne, who was two years older, in F3.

Senna's lay-off had also meant he missed the Formula Ford Festival, one that Van Diemen would have expected him to enter. The 'lottery' element of the Festival, which could see a reputation broken due to a misplaced wheel or a simple mechanical problem, perhaps kept him away. Senna didn't need to do it: he had won everything going, and it wouldn't be beyond the realms of possibility that someone with his ruthless and intransigent nature suddenly headed for the hills without warning, phone off the hook.

And yet he was still fuming that Byrne, as a salaried driver (Senna had to fund his own drive) had won the festival in his absence, using his chassis to boot.

Tommy wasn't impressed with 'rich, pain-in-the-arse Senna da Silva' – who he described as being 'more arrogant than me' and it is believed Senna wasn't too impressed with him either!

Senna would contest the 1982 season in Formula Ford 2000 driving a Van Diemen car again, but in this category the cars were run by Dennis Rushen and Robin Green.

This category didn't quite have the attraction of FF1600, and Senna was never really seriously challenged.

On the way to a round in Denmark, at which he could clinch the title, Senna chatted to Keith Sutton about many things, including the breakdown of his marriage. He also had a proposition for him:

'We discussed him going to F1 and me being his photographer,' remembers Keith:

> He would pay my salary, air fares, expenses: when it actually came to it at the start of 1984, he asked me to do that and I wasn't prepared to do it. First of all I wanted to start an agency – the other side of it is that by employing me he would have owned the copyright on all the pictures. He'd already told me I was only allowed to photograph him – if he's paying me, that's all he wanted. If I went to race, I'd have to be sat at a corner, waiting for him and clicking the shutter when he came round and as a photographer that's not too inspiring, as much as it was an honour to be asked. I always think that he wasn't used to people saying no to him.

Senna did clinch the title in Denmark, which led to the famous evening spent with Keith and his camera as he rolled around the bars and clubs in celebration of his title. Even when it came to matters outside motor racing, he remained competitive.

The aforementioned – and superbly named – Calvin Fish was also there. Sutton recalls. 'There was this one girl they both took a shine to. It was quite funny to watch them battling it out for her attentions.'

Whether or not Senna, whose slight physique and lack of hardcore boozing experience meant he was four sheets to the wind as soon as he walked into the pub, won the battle for this particular young lady is not documented. He nevertheless didn't go home empty-handed, and told Sutton, who had followed him into his hotel room, to clear off!

1983: Formula 3

As the European Formula Ford champion, Senna's next step was the British Formula 3 championship.

He signed to drive for New Zealander Dick Bennetts' West Surrey Racing Team, an outfit that had already guided Jonathan Palmer and Stefan Johansson to the crown and would go on to achieve great success with drivers such as Mika Hakkinen and Rubens Barrichello in later years.

His performances in the category left no doubt as to his ability and Senna won the first nine races on the trot to establish a colossal lead in the title chase.

Senna's star in Britain ascended a little further when it emerged that his main rival for the title was Norfolk's Martin Brundle, driving for Eddie Jordan Racing. The Englishman had started the season slowly but soon began to assert himself against the younger Brazilian.

Brundle first began to get on top of Senna at Silverstone when a last-minute change to softer, European-championship spec tyres put him on pole, ahead of the Brazilian who was on the same rubber. Senna crashed trying to keep up. He also crashed heavily at Cadwell Park the next week during qualifying, and at a race at Snetterton he was enraged when the pair clashed and he felt he had been assailed by his rival.

He went as far as lodging a protest, having either forgotten or been unaware that Snetteron was Brundle's stomping ground. His complaints were not upheld, and he, as he would again, fumed that the system had conspired against him.

At Oulton Park, Senna tried a kamikaze lunge up the inside of the Brit even though he was almost a full car-length behind and ended up with his Ralt parked on top of Brundle's, just missing Martin's head.

To his credit Senna's first action was to peer out of his cockpit and check he had merely run his rival off the road, not bumped him as well. This was the driver as he would always be – relentless to the point of being dangerous, albeit always careful to check on the plight of his victims! *The Mail on Sunday* had been sufficiently interested by events in the championship to send their reporter Malcolm Folley there.

The chagrined Brundle told him, 'It should have been my race, instead all I've got is tyre marks from Senna's car down my helmet.'

Many years later, Brundle told Folley a story he says is a perfect summation of the talent Ayrton Senna had behind the wheel of a racing car.

At another soaking race at Silverstone, Brundle was heading into Stowe on the first lap in the lead, only to have Senna bomb round the outside of him. Brundle was unperturbed, feeling that his rival and the crash barrier were about to have an unscheduled rendezvous, but Senna made the move stick.

When Brundle tried the same thing the next time round, it didn't work and he skidded clean off the track. How come?

Senna told Brundle on the podium he had known, first time round, there was enough detritus on the track – bits of old rubber and so forth – to give him sufficient grip. Next time round, he realised there was now too much water and this trick wouldn't work. How did he know? He just did. Brundle was an incredulous and impressed second.

There was also the famous story of Senna taping over his radiator outlet to get his engine up to optimum temperature far quicker than any of the other competitors. Of course, if the tape remained fastened then the engine would have detonated itself. So, after a lap and with stopping power at full tilt, Senna undid his belts, leaned out, and removed the tape himself.

As the season progressed, Brundle started to claw back the deficit to Senna, and at one point was actually ahead of him in the standings.

Senna never took a disadvantage lying down and was beginning to have his suspicions that the Toyota engine in the back of his Ralt chassis was past its best. One snag: it had been prepared by a company called Novamotor, in Italy. While many may have taken this setback on the chin, Senna wasn't going to let the small matter of geographical distance stand between him and the F3 title. So what did he do? He loaded the engine into the back of his trusty Alfasud and drove all the way south for a replacement, and it paid off: the 23 year old from Santana was crowned a deserving champion at the first time of asking with one race remaining in Macau.

The stars of this race, being run to Formula 3 specifications for the first time, have long since become venerated in the same manner as Grand Prix drivers who excel at Monaco. Senna was to prove to be no exception, although his preparations for the race weren't exactly textbook.

Mike Doodson first met Senna in 1983 when he was asked by *Autosport* to cover the Macau event.

'He arrived the night before practice', remembers Mike. 'He put it on pole and because it was his last with West Surrey Racing and Dick Bennetts, he decided to go out and celebrate. He got stuck into the vodka, which he did on a number of occasions. It wasn't the first time. He did everything to its maximum, which included drinking vodka. He went to bed with a very sore head, and he still had it when he woke up. He did a couple of laps on Saturday morning and then went back to bed. He ducked out of some sponsor things, went back to bed and slept, and that sorted him out. He won the race quite handily the following day.'

That must have been rather defeating for his rivals: even when he was hung over, they couldn't stop him.

1984: Toleman and Formula 1

With Senna's success in the junior formulae, it was a matter of when rather than if he would ascend to the top tier of motoring competition.

The first time he drove F1 machinery, a Williams–Cosworth FW08C, was as the result of a happy coincidence: Senna had found himself stationed beside team boss Frank Williams on a flight and had spent the duration bending his ear about how good he was, with the result that Frank agreed to give him a go in one of his cars.

So Senna arrived at Donington Park on Tuesday 19 July 1983, to see what all the fuss was about.

This was a very informal affair indeed: Senna showed up with his West Surrey Racing overalls and helmet and the car itself was still equipped with reigning champion Keke Rosberg's fitted seat and number 1 decal on the nosecone. Williams had no intention at all of signing Senna for 1984 as he had Rosberg and multiple race-winner Jacques Laffite on his books, but still there is little doubt he was doing it for his own benefit as much as Senna's.

Senna was immediately on the pace and finished the day with 83 laps under his belt, the fastest one second inside the car's previous best. And that was that. The driver thanked the Williams staff, got into his car, and left.

Senna was often in touch with Frank and his wife Ginny and would meet them for dinner quite a lot in his early days. On one occasion when he was doing the driving to the appointed restaurant, he was apparently so engrossed in conversation he drove down the middle of the road at 25mph in top gear, his Alfa's little 1300cc coughing and spluttering.

Williams demanded of him, 'Do you always drive like a w****r?'

A funny thing, in hindsight, to ask Ayrton Senna.

Senna was also granted a test by McLaren, who were assessing Brundle and German hotshot Stefan Bellof the same day. All three men were given a benchmark time by outgoing driver John Watson and were all quickly under it. On Senna's final run the Ford V8 blew. Rather than apologising to Ron Dennis, as some may have expected him to do, he asked him what time he had done. Dennis's answer was something along the lines of 'I find it hard to care about pressing the button on a stopwatch when one of my cars is disintegrating in front of me.'

Senna did not feel that he had demonstrated his superiority over Brundle and Bellof and badgered Dennis to give him another go when a new Cosworth had been installed. Inevitably, he was quicker: his natural speed being made doubly evident by his intense will to be the best.

Senna was also to test for Brabham-BMW, the home of world champion Nelson Piquet, and the less well-rated Toleman outfit.

It was conceivable that Senna could have replaced Riccardo Patrese at the team, but Piquet wasn't so keen on the idea. In retrospect, there can be little doubt that at this stage of his career Senna might have become the victim of the kind of controlled hostility he used to such great effect on his own teammates in succeeding years.

'In seven years with [main team sponsor] Parmalat,' Bernie Ecclestone, Brabham's owner at the time, remembers, 'the only time Piquet spoke to them was 15 conversations in three days when we were thinking of Senna for the second car.'

After testing for the four outfits, Senna went for Toleman-Hart: a team heading for the top bit by bit. His decision to go there was borne of a combination of factors: while many years later Lewis Hamilton would see his decision to kick-start his F1 career in the same team as a double world champion vindicated, it is tough to argue that such a move is without its risks.

'He needed a year of apprenticeship in F1 and Toleman was the team best placed to offer him that,' says Doodson. 'They had good engineers and a decent budget and like him, were on the up and looking to do better.'

The team had commenced their Formula 1 operation in 1981 as the brainchild of businessman Ted Toleman and his partner Alex Hawkridge. They had struggled to make an impression with an overweight and underdeveloped car in their début season and the promising Derek Warwick only succeeded in qualifying for one round. As time progressed, the cars remained somewhat unrefined, but the team's undeniable engineering pedigree made its presence felt: both Rory Byrne and Pat Symonds would eventually be major players in a total of seventeen world championships for Benetton, Ferrari and Renault and the team steadily improved. Warwick had challenged Didier Pironi for second position at the 1982 British Grand Prix (despite driving a TG182 memorably described by Clive James as having 'the power to weight ratio of the Barbican Arts Centre') and in 1983 the team scored their first points at Zandvoort.

Pre-season testing gave Senna an opportunity to acquaint himself with not only the machinery but the tyres he would be using in the season ahead. Senna was not a man given to blending into the background – despite having never turned the wheel of a

Grand Prix car in a competitive setting he let the Pirelli engineers know what he felt was lacking in their product.

Doodson reminisces, 'I was walking around the back of the pits and will never forget the sound of this voice, quite high, speaking Italian, and I knew it was Senna. I looked in the back of the garage and he was with Mario Mezzanotte, the chief engineer for Pirelli, and a couple of other guys, telling them what was wrong with their tyres. This is a lad who had never raced an F1 car and had only done one day of testing in a brand new car, on their tyres and he was telling them what was wrong. And he was right!'

Meanwhile, it was all change at the front for the 1984 F1 season. The main protagonists from the past two seasons – Williams, Brabham, Renault and Ferrari – were largely reduced to bit players, with only four wins between them over the course of the 16 races.

McLaren's drivers, under the stewardship of the determined Ron Dennis, suddenly found themselves elevated from the ignominy of the previous year to the front of the field, and in some style.

Niki Lauda, who had endured a barren 1983, was paired with Frenchman Alain Prost who had been given the heave-ho by Renault after losing the title to Piquet. The two had found themselves gifted the best car in the field, the TAG-Porsche powered MP4–2, which was ridiculously superior in race conditions if not necessarily qualifying.

Meanwhile followers of the British F3 scrap the previous year would have been keeping their eyes on the two débutantes as they lined up on the grid for Round One in Rio de Janeiro.

In 17th position on the start line, the lumpy number 19 car of the reigning British F3 champion was five seconds off the pace but destined for better things in the race itself. Senna's new teammate Johnny Cecotto, no slouch, having been a 350cc world motorcycling champion in 1975 and F2 runner-up in

1982, was only one place behind on the grid, and yet the local boy was ahead of him by a whopping 1.775 seconds.

Martin Brundle, meanwhile, had qualified on the row behind but in the race he finished fifth and scored two points on his world championship bow. Senna, on the other hand, retired after eight laps with turbo failure.

At Kyalami, the next race, Senna made it to the finish but found the demands of hustling Grand Prix machinery around the sweeping track to be very different from whizzing about Snetterton in an F3 car.

He was utterly exhausted and suffering from muscular spasms in his neck when he trundled back to the Toleman pit, leading his reverential mechanics to dub him 'the Wimp'.

Senna, uneasy with the level of pain he was suffering, apparently had to be reassured by Sid Watkins that he wasn't at death's door! His talent was from the top drawer, but his physical fitness needed some fine tuning to keep up.

Senna finished in the points at Zolder, and although at Imola his confidence took a minor dent when, for the first and only time in his F1 career, he failed to qualify for a Grand Prix after both fuel pressure and tyre issues, this was as bad as things became. At the start of June, the circus paid its annual visit to the streets of Monte Carlo.

Many of the sport's greatest drivers announce themselves with a signature performance early in their career, one that grabs the attention of the headline writers and the wider world in one fell swoop. Michael Schumacher didn't hang about and managed it in his first ever race by qualifying seventh at Spa-Francorchamps. Gilles Villeneuve won his home Grand Prix in torrential conditions in his first full season. In the modern era, Sebastian Vettel, even when he didn't have the best chassis on the grid at his disposal, dominated at a slippery Monza in 2008, making the established runners look amateur in comparison. And Monaco 1984 was about one man: Ayrton Senna.

Monaco is often seen as the great leveller of Grand Prix racing. The circuit is highly incongruous in the company of super-sleek motordromes like Sakhir and Istanbul Park (read into that what you will) and it is often said that if the president of the Automobile Club de Monaco approached Bernie Ecclestone with the idea for the race these days, he'd barely have time to take the plans out of his briefcase before the men in *les manteaux blancs* arrived to escort him off the premises.

The circuit's minuscule confines place more emphasis on car control and driver skill than out-and-out car performance, although a nimble chassis helps. So it has been the case, many times, that the greatest drivers have transcended their machinery to record impressive results there.

The Monaco Grand Prix had seen both rain and unusual results in the previous two years. Riccardo Patrese had won in 1982 even though he had spun and stalled on the final lap, and in 1983 Keke Rosberg had started on slicks and blown away the opposition, all of whom to a man had started on rain tyres.

This time the wet-weather rubber was a formality and the tunnel under the Lowes Hotel was artificially watered so it could cope with what would otherwise have been unfriendly dry asphalt. Senna, now equipped with Toleman's new car, was thirteenth on the grid.

In the early stages, attention was elsewhere. Nigel Mansell slung his Lotus past Prost's McLaren and scampered, if that verb could ever be applied to someone of Mansell's build, away at two seconds a lap. It may have appeared as though he was in an inordinate hurry. Then no sooner had Mansell begun thinking about how best to bow to Prince Rainier, he was off, his rear wheel having kissed a painted line on the road. Nigel got out of the bent car and aimed a grumpy kick at his right rear tyre by way of revenge.

This left Prost back in the lead, but further down the field things were happening. Lauda was overtaken by a white and yellow blur as he motored past the pits, on the outside no less. The blur turned out to be Senna, who was now closing in Prost at a rate of knots.

To make proceedings even more interesting for him, his Hart engine's turbo lag was so bad round the streets of the Principality he simply changed up before the turbo cut in, which robbed him of horsepower but helped keep the car on the road.

As the rain continued to fall, Prost decided he had had enough for the afternoon. He had been the man whose car launched his friend Didier Pironi into the trees during practice at Hockenheim in 1982, in a crash that had almost cost the Ferrari driver his legs. Since that day he had always disliked the rain – not for the slippery surface, with which he had no problem, but because he couldn't see where he was going. Senna, with a race to win and no such circumspection holding him back, kept his foot down.

Prost was soon gesticulating to the stewards to have the race stopped. He got his wish at the start of lap 33 and immediately parked his McLaren, just as Senna roared past into the lead.

Clerk of the course that day was Jacky Ickx, an ex-F1 driver of some repute and a man who had won Le Mans no less than six times. Ickx, as a Francophone and a regular Porsche driver, was accused of ensuring that the Porsche-propelled Prost got his wish. The results were counted back to the previous lap and The Professor took the win, something that keeps the conspiracy theorists grumbling to this day.

Ironically, Ickx did Prost the greatest possible disservice as the curtailment of the race before full distance meant only half-points were awarded. Prost's 4.5 points, as opposed to the full nine he could have earned, contributed to him losing the world title to Niki Lauda later in the year by half a point. F1 can be a cruel business.

Senna, however, took his narrow defeat philosophically and accepted he had finished in second place, although he had driven his slowing-down lap waving at the crowd in the manner of a man who thought otherwise. Nevertheless, the F1 world now knew this was no run-of-the-mill rookie.

This was to be the first of the thirty-eight times we would see Prost and Senna together on the podium, and neither of them looked particularly delighted. This was also not the last time (or even the first) Senna would feel that the 'system' had gone against him.

It should be highlighted, for the few unaware of the circumstances, that the race did not simply announce Senna's arrival as a top-flight racing driver. It is a measure of how hindsight can apportion greater significance to an event in light of later developments that Senna's début at Monaco is now seen as evidence that he was destined for success, whereas Tyrrell's Stefan Bellof – who himself was to die in a brutal head on crash, racing at Spa in the World Sportscar Championship, before he attained the reputation he deserved – was closing on Senna faster than Senna was closing on Prost. Had the race run its course, Prost would surely not have won, but arguably neither would Senna. It was also believed by some that Senna's very obvious clouting of the kerb at the chicane as he hunted down the leader would have spelled suspension failure for his TG184 before the chequered flag fell.

Still, as the year wore on the progress being made by the Toleman team was evident. No longer did they need a soaking circuit to show well, as underlined not only by Senna's heroics but by the performances of his on-off teammate Stefan Johansson, drafted in to replace Cecotto, who had broken his legs. At a dry Brands Hatch Senna finished third behind Lauda and Warwick, and at the Austrian Grand Prix Senna rocketed from tenth to fourth at the start.

A rather comedic snapshot of Senna's time with Toleman is provided by the *Autosport* report of the 1984 Dallas Grand Prix, the first and, as it transpired, only running of the race. It was a farcical affair from start to finish, with legal wrangles, appalling organisation, a track made of cornflakes and a bunch of grumpy drivers all adding to the Benny Hill atmosphere. The usual order was turned on its head, and the Toleman was arguably the best-handling car on the circuit. In qualifying Senna did well, aided by a novel method of keeping cool in the near-forty degree heat. Given his exhaustion problems in South Africa, his mechanics had emptied a freezer's worth of ice down his overalls.

Unfortunately this perhaps relaxed him rather too much as he then forgot to fasten his helmet straps properly and, as he hit the brakes for the first time, it slipped over his eyes. Hanna–Barbera would have been proud. The race was little better as he made a rookie's mistake and spun the car into the wall on the second lap. In his defence, his crotch straps had made his legs numb, and his driveshaft eventually disintegrated.

The driver and team were nevertheless rumbling along nicely in their first year together and Alex Hawkridge must have been gleefully anticipating what lay ahead in 1985. But when the Italian Grand Prix rolled around in September Senna would not be participating.

Having decided that the Toleman team could not offer him the kind of machinery or results to which he felt his talent should be married, Senna opened negotiations with Team Lotus, not necessarily an obvious choice given that at that time it was two years without a win, not since the death of Colin Chapman, and six years without a championship.

However, Gerard Ducarouge was regarded as a star designer and his 95T had shown well throughout the season, with Mansell and Elio de Angelis demonstrating the car had raw speed when it felt like it.

All well and good. But the caveat to all this was that Senna was still contracted to Alex Hawkridge and, to make matters worse, had conducted the negotiations with Peter Warr in a rather clandestine manner. Senna was indeed allowed to talk to other teams, but he was obliged to be totally open about it and he had not been.

19th July 1983. Even though this was Senna's first taste of F1 machinery he was already fully applying himself to the task in hand.

Ayrton enjoys some rare time away from the track at home in Esher with his model helicopter.

Senna, seen here climbing Eau Rouge in the Belgian Grand Prix of 1986, and the nimble Lotus-Renault were a fearsome combination.

Senna and Alain Prost – probably the two most famous rivals in the history of motorsport – enjoyed a cordial relationship in their first year at McLaren, but it deteriorated spectacularly the following season.

A shaken Senna discusses the horrific crash that befell Lotus's Martin Donnelly with his good friend, the late Prof Sid Watkins, at Jerez in 1990.

Following their clash at Suzuka the previous year, Senna and Prost are at it again in 1990. On this occasion it was Senna who triumphed in the World Championship, later admitting this collision had been deliberate.

Senna cuts through the field in astonishing fashion at a rain soaked Donington Park on Easter Sunday 1993. On the opening lap of the race he went from fifth to first.

An unhappy marriage. Senna hustles the recalcitrant Williams FW16 around Imola on the last weekend of his life.

Incensed, Hawkridge told Senna he would not be driving at Monza. Senna, as was his way, felt that he was the wronged party and the TV cameras caught him dressed in his civvies and waving his arms around on the pit wall as he tried to explain himself.

Senna and Hawkridge had bumped foreheads before then. Earlier in the year Senna was left aghast and in tears when Hawkridge gave him a grilling for failing to inform him that he would be wearing personal sponsor patches on his overalls. He was allowed to, but he had to say so first! But the punishment at Monza was much worse than being ticked off: for Senna being prevented from driving was tantamount to cutting off a limb.

Stefan Johansson found himself leading the team in Senna's absence, and brought his car home a very respectable fourth. Perhaps the team didn't need Senna any more than he needed them.

'I wasn't surprised that he went to Lotus,' says Mike Doodson:

I was well aware of the fact that he was a guy who didn't mind how many toes he stepped on on the way up, because you were sure that he would never need the help of those people on the way down. He made the assumption that when he announced he was going to Lotus, Toleman would invoke the financial penalty and they would part with decent grace. What Toleman were upset by was the fact that they had invested a lot of money in this young driver and they were expecting to have him the following year because he hadn't said anything to the contrary.

The fact is that he had the right to do what he did, it's just that he didn't tell Toleman about it, and it left them looking a bit stupid. It was foolishness on his part, but I don't think it was a deliberate snub.

Senna himself was apparently far from impressed: 'The whole thing at Zandvoort was disgusting. I was very annoyed with [Lotus boss] Peter Warr ... it was my desire and duty as a professional to inform Toleman that I was leaving,' which, if true, backs up Doodson's assertions.

As it turned out, Toleman didn't even make the first few rounds of 1985 after running into tyre supply troubles with Michelin, who left the sport, so Senna did the right thing.

Another podium followed, behind the two McLarens, at the season-ending Portuguese race held at the newly-revamped Estoril track. Senna, having qualified a magnificent third, was on for a strong second after the retirement of Nigel Mansell but was passed by Niki Lauda towards the end of the race as the Austrian threw caution, and fuel economy, to the winds in his effort to land his third world title. He succeeded.

That year, 1984, acted as something of a snapshot of the Senna experience: breathtaking racing in the wet, transcendence of equipment and an unshakeable, almost selfish approach to the politics of the sport.

6

Lotus Flowers

1985: Rain Dance at Estoril

Over the winter of 1984 –1985, Senna had a minor health scare when he contracted a virus that left half his face drooping in a manner that might have been comical were it not a cause for alarm. Thankfully the temporary palsy cleared up in time for him to slot himself into the black and gold cockpit of the JPS Lotus for the first race of 1985. He was also sporting the logo of a Brazilian bank, Nacional, a logo that would become synonymous with him for the rest of his career.

Senna now had a car worthy of his talents and it was not long before he put it to use.

Ayrton had been superb at the Portuguese Autodromo do Estoril in 1984, but six months on for Round Two he was something else again.

Qualifying delivered Senna the first of what would turn out to be 65 pole positions, and fate, or God, smiled on him as on Sunday the skies erupted.

In his race report in *Autosport,* Nigel Roebuck wrote: 'Just occasionally comes a race when one driver makes the rest look ordinary, and this was one such.'

It certainly was. From the very start, Senna made the best use of his relatively clear field of vision and powered away in the lead, initially followed by his teammate de Angelis.

Conditions became even worse as the race approached the end and Senna thought it was about time he wrapped his win up and headed inside for a warm blanket. He decided to emulate a tactic used to great effect by Prost at Monaco the previous year and started waving his arm at the stewards. This time, the gesturing was not heeded.

One can see why Senna was probably clock-watching as the race ran to the maximum allowable time of two hours. When the chequered flag fell, the number 12 Lotus was a whopping sixty-two seconds clear of the second-placed finisher Michele Alboreto.

The McLarens were nowhere to be seen, Prost in particular having aquaplaned off the track backwards and deprived his car of its rear wing, no doubt to the chagrin of Marlboro who lost 20 per cent of their advertising.

As at Monaco the year before, Senna was punching the air and waving in delight as he rounded the circuit on his slowing-down lap but this time the celebrations were merited. He had achieved a clean sweep: pole position, fastest lap and a dominant race win in only his sixteenth Grand Prix start, whilst the others all around him looked flat-footed. Peter Warr, standing in front of the car like a proud father welcoming a gold star child home from school, looked as thrilled as Senna. This was not a race; this was a display of dominance.

Interestingly the victor did not feel that it had been a perfect performance. Senna rarely admitted to his mistakes, but he was on occasion exceedingly modest about his most impressive performances.

> The big danger was that the conditions changed all the time. Sometimes the rain was very heavy, sometimes not. I couldn't see anything behind me. It was difficult even to keep the car in a straight line, and for sure the race should have been stopped. Once I nearly spun in front of the pits, like Prost, and I was lucky to stay on the road. People think I made no mistakes but that's not true – I've no idea

how many times I went off! Once I had all four wheels on the grass, totally out of control, but the car came back onto the circuit.

On the day that Brazil's first elected president Tancredo Neves had died, Senna gave the Brazilian nation something to smile about, and it wouldn't be the last time.

In 1985 Senna took the first of his five career poles at Monaco, the scene of his heartbreak twelve months before, but his ethics were called into question when some rivals accused him of deliberately driving slowly to stop them bettering his qualifying time.

Regardless, Senna retired early with engine issues and then in Canada was unusually bested by de Angelis, who outqualified him by three tenths of a second to claim pole. Again, he was pointless at the finish and then made an error in Detroit, when he skidded off on the marbles at the second corner while trying to overtake Alboreto, and slammed into the wall.

There was a scary accident at Paul Ricard when the Renault engine, overwhelmed by the pressure to perform well in front of a home crowd, blew and sent Senna's car through the perimeter catch fencing at high speed. It could not have chosen a more dangerous place to surrender: Senna was bombing down the Mistral straight into the Signes corner when it happened. He was lucky he went in backwards – had things been different disaster would have resulted. Watching a replay of this incident now emphasises the huge strides made in safety since then. The worst thing likely to happen if a driver runs wide now is that he might leave unsightly tyre marks on the logo of whichever company has sponsored the giant tarmac run-off areas.

Silverstone was another duffer as Senna's electronics gave up the ghost with five laps to go, and at the Nurburgring Teo Fabi surprisingly gave the returning Toleman team what Senna hadn't managed to do a year before: a pole position. Senna only qualified fifth and then retired once more.

It wasn't until Austria that Senna notched his second points finish of the season, with a combative second after an extremely lowly fourteenth on the grid, and then followed that up with third at Zandvoort behind the charging McLarens, Niki Lauda bringing the curtain down on his illustrious career with his twenty-fifth and final win.

Senna added a second win to his tally at Spa-Francorchamps later that year.

The permanent home of the Belgian Grand Prix from 1985 onwards, Spa is renowned for its inclement and unpredictable weather, not helped by its late-August slot in the F1 calendar. In 1985 the race was rescheduled for the late spring, as it had been in 1983, seemingly upsetting the natural order of things. As if confused, the sunshine baked the newly-laid 'all-weather' asphalt until it melted. Although Senna would probably still have given the race his best shot, even if he had to drive each lap in a constant forty-five degree drift, he didn't have the chance as the event was postponed until September. By then, the normal Spa service (and surface) had been restored and Senna romped to his second win in slippery conditions.

He was so content with his win at the ultimate drivers' track that he decided to do an impromptu lap of honour at the end, ignoring the marshals imploring him to dive into the pits.

By now the admiration with which Senna was held by his peers was growing. At the European Grand Prix, Ulsterman John Watson returned to his old McLaren team to deputise for Niki Lauda, who had broken his wrist in a practice accident at Spa. During practice Watson, a pretty decent pedaller himself in his day (he still holds the record for winning a Grand Prix from furthest back on the grid) was overtaken by Senna.

He later recalled, 'He came through at Dingle Dell. I sat there gobsmacked. That car to me was like rain dancing off a pavement.

He had control of the car yet had it running in a way that was just … I thought well, there's clear signal that my time as a Grand Prix driver was effectively finished, because I realised at that point, here was a man doing things that I hadn't even thought of, let alone put into effect.'

The Lotus 97T was a solid, sleek car with a decent engine but in the races it could prove an untrustworthy steed.

Overall 1985 was a year that promised much but delivered less. Although it was a dramatic improvement from 1984 and a mark of unquestionable progress, Senna was not a serious championship challenger. He notched up seven pole positions but only converted two of those into victories, dogged by poor reliability.

With greater prominence also came greater controversy. Senna was now at the sharp end of the grid and getting up the noses of world champions. One such nose belonged to Keke Rosberg. During the European Grand Prix at Brands Hatch, Senna chopped him up whilst contending the lead and sent Rosberg spinning off the circuit. When he later encountered the Lotus, the Finn deliberately made a thorough nuisance of himself and blocked Senna with the subtlety of a wrecking ball, allowing his teammate Nigel Mansell to escape to his first win.

There were still the occasional signs of an inexperienced driver too; at Adelaide, Senna was all over the place, running off the road and damaging his front wing as well as running his tyres down to the canvas as he again battled with Keke Rosberg's victorious Williams.

'The problem with Ayrton is that he is very talented and very fast but he is just going too hard,' said Rosberg, a sentiment that was echoed by his teammate Mansell, who had clashed with the Lotus at the start.

'Senna was a total idiot to drive me off the road like that,' he raged, adding somewhat bemusingly, 'He might be quick, he might be good, but he is not a good driver.'

1986: John Player's Special Ingredient

The Warwick affair sullied Senna's reputation over the close season, but he remained unbowed by the criticism. He had clearly established himself as the fastest if not necessarily the most polished competitor in the sport, and certainly the number one driver at Lotus. This did not go down at all well with Elio de Angelis, who had been with the team since the Chapman days and was wondering how this new guy could have pulled the rug from under his feet. Senna rallied the troops about him when de Angelis wasn't looking, in the same manner he would do again at McLaren when he brought 'Prost's team' round to his way of thinking.

'Senna had de Angelis sorted out right from the get-go. It destroyed him. He was superior only once, in Canada,' says Mike Doodson.

> I got some good quotes from Nigel Stepney, who was a mechanic on both cars. He started with de Angelis, who he'd been with since the Shadow days [1979 onwards], and the two of them had a very close relationship. Senna wangled it that Stepney and his guys would work on his car instead of de Angelis. De Angelis was very upset about that. It's another example of, you could call it ruthless-ness, but it seems only practical that the bloke who is setting the lap times and is doing well in the races should also have the reliability that comes from having the better crew of mechanics.

De Angelis gave his version of events to *Grand Prix International* at the time, being careful to have a parting swipe at his ex-colleague: 'I was put on one side by Lotus. All they could think about was Senna. I knew that he would be a difficult person, of course. I admired his determination and he is very determined – maybe too much. That kind of driving doesn't always pay off.'

De Angelis departed to Brabham to partner Riccardo Patrese, an altogether less political animal, whereas Senna now had what he wanted in Johnny Dumfries: a teammate who would not demand parity of equipment.

The Lotus' Renault engine, featuring compressed air instead of valve springs, was good but also rather more avaricious than Williams's Honda and McLaren's TAG units. With fuel tightly restricted for the new season emphasis was placed on efficiency and rather often Lotus's rivals could simply afford to crank up the boost and drive past.

This, in turn, had a knock-on effect on the amount of time devoted to tweaking the 98T chassis as all the testing was devoted to ensuring every last drop of fuel was put to proper use by the engine. In Senna's three years at Lotus it is arguable that the car itself got worse each year, at least in terms of development if not design.

In Brazil the cheers for Senna in the grandstands were louder than for Piquet, which writer Jeff Hutchinson, in attendance, attributed to 'underdog syndrome'. Senna had pole position again but was bested by the crowd's second-favourite driver in a far superior car.

While this was doubtless a welcome tonic for team owner Frank Williams, convalescing after a pre-season crash that left him in a wheelchair for the rest of his life, the driver of his other car enjoyed a *contretemps* with the crowd's new favourite.

On the first lap Nigel Mansell tried to overtake Senna as they headed towards a left-hand corner. Senna simply ran the Williams off the road as the Englishman tried to squeeze by, Mansell later said 'We did not talk about it afterwards, but I learned an important lesson about racing against him that day. If I hadn't backed off we would both have hit the Armco and it could have been a serious accident. As it was I came off worse and it would not happen again. His tactic was to intimidate and I refused to be intimidated.'

'Senna, it is hardly a secret, has a somewhat exclusive fan club when it comes to his fellow drivers,' wrote Nigel Roebuck in *Autosport*. 'Senna seems to make his own rules,' one driver muttered to me, 'so perhaps we'll all have to play by them ...'

However, there was no controversy at the second round, the first Spanish Grand Prix since 1981 and the inaugural race at the new Jerez circuit. Senna was on pole again, as ever, but in the race the Williams was miles ahead – in performance terms at least.

Mansell, after a tyre stop, dropped right down the order but had grip to give away. Apparently remembering his pledge to remain unintimidated by Senna, he overtook everyone ahead and was reeling in the Lotus hand over fist. Out of the final corner, Mansell was in Senna's slipstream and jinked out to the right to pass, but he didn't have enough road. The finish line was located further back than the start line at the new circuit and, had the two been in the same position, Mansell would almost definitely have won. As it was, Senna took the spoils by 0.014 of a second – or about the length of a nosecone.

Senna afterwards said that his Goodyears were absolutely finished, and he had been doing everything in his power to 'play around' to find the grip available to him: his skill in slippery conditions didn't just serve him well in the wet!

Prost, who hadn't made life easy for Mansell as he climbed back through the field, afterwards apologised to him, saying, 'I'd have let you through if I thought you'd have beaten Ayrton.'

Senna's hair's-breadth victory remained, until the farcical US Grand Prix of 2002, the second-closest win in history behind the 1971 Italian Grand Prix.

There was a sombre atmosphere at Spa as the paddock struggled to deal with the death of Elio de Angelis at a testing accident at Paul Ricard. In the race Senna came in for some stiff criticism – the blame for a first-corner collision was pinned on him. As he rocketed off into the distance, unscathed, there were some who christened him the 'Teflon man' – much as Fernando

Alonso would be named twenty years later but for different reasons. Alain Prost lost the most in the fracas and launched a stunning recovery drive from last place, while Mansell won his first race of the year and sent his apologies to Frank Williams for taking so long to open his '86 account.

In Canada, Prost completed an unusually forceful, albeit fair move on his new rival, perhaps spurred, it was speculated, by what had happened in Belgium. Senna's reaction when asked if he thought the manoeuvre was quite different to what it would have been in subsequent years:

'No, it was quite fair. Hard, but fair,' he admitted. He had also suffered the ignominy of being lapped by winner Mansell after technical troubles.

Come qualifying in Detroit, Senna appeared, for once, to have things other than Formula 1 on his mind. Senna was a big Corinthians fan, but this was even more important than a mere club match: Brazil vs France at Mexico '86. He set pole position on Friday but the next day was unable to go faster. No sooner had his V6 stopped turning than Senna was barricaded into his hotel room, inches away from the TV screen. Outside the Americans, unfussed about soccer and also unused to sports stars not doing their publicity work, were unimpressed. So when France beat the South Americans 5–4, sympathetic figures were few and far between, and Senna later admitted he didn't dare face his Renault engineers after the game.

On Sunday, perhaps spurred on by a desire to salvage some national and personal pride, Senna drove like he had scorpions down his trousers, climbing back up the field after dropping to eighth as a result of a deflating tyre to record his fourth win. In the process he returned Mansell's favour from the week before and put a lap on him before the flag. His winning margin was more than 30 seconds.

He was interviewed for the Brazilian panel programme *Roda Viva* in the immediate aftermath of the race, giving a rare glimpse into the less intense side of his persona, being reduced to tears by a musical film of his most recent victory.

'Do you know what song was playing?' he was asked by one panelist.

Senna shook his head.

'Boys Don't Cry!'

'Do you always cry?' asked another.

'I wasn't crying!' came the retort, as its source wiped his eyes.

Senna, for reasons best known to the producers of the programme, was sketched by a caricaturist as he talked. When he was made aware of this, he grinned and covered his ears, made slightly more prominent by the shorter hairstyle he favoured at the time.

'Take it easy with my aerodynamics!'

In France, Senna, as in 1985, unbelievably slid out of the Grand Prix at Signes corner. Although he skidded on oil dropped by Andrea de Cesaris' Minardi, he was unusually self-critical, whereas in reality, de Cesaris was almost entirely to blame – his cheerful and clueless dithering around the circuit, spraying lubricant on the tarmac, eliciting customary head-shakes among the parade of watching journalists.

Before the British Grand Prix in 1986, Murray Walker, commentating on a shot of Senna standing beside his Lotus having a drink, described him as the 'serious Ayrton Senna'. At the very same moment Senna grinned and waved to the camera, before pretending to throttle his mechanic as he helped him clamber into the cockpit. Another Murray-ism for the canon.

At the start of the race, Frenchman Jacques Laffite was involved in a pile-up at Paddock Hill bend that left him with two broken legs. It was a sad end to a career that had seen Laffite challenge for the championship in 1981 and enjoy a minirenaissance in 1986, with a podium in Brazil among other strong showings.

Senna, meanwhile, retired after struggling with, as Clive James put it, 'a gearbox that would sometimes select fourth and sometimes BBC2'.

Hockenheim, like Imola, placed a premium on fuel economy and Senna's ill-deserved reputation as a flat-out, tyre-chewing fuel-gulper was belied somewhat in Germany when he finished second after driving a careful, conservative race. He did, however, cut it fine and had to weave from side to side to slosh the dregs of petrol into the fuel pick-up. The usual exponent of this careful approach, Prost, ran out of fuel and tried and failed to push his McLaren over the line after coughing to a halt within sight of the flag, to cheers from the crowd. He was not impressed.

The circus visited the Hungaroring for the first time two weeks later. The tight and slippery new circuit – like Monaco without the houses, as Murray Walker remarked, was the venue for the first Grand Prix to be held behind the Iron Curtain. The race provided entertainment for the curious onlookers, who numbered over 200,000. Despite having a nasty surprise in practice when he nearly collided with a course car that was removing Patrese's marooned Brabham from a kerb, as well as five spins in three days, Senna took pole.

In the race itself, he fought a famous battle with Nelson Piquet. Piquet, premiering a new differential (of which he conveniently forgot to inform Nigel Mansell), had a much superior car underneath him and yet Senna hung in there, pulling some wondrous laps out of the bag on old rubber, as he had done in Jerez, when Piquet was in the pits to offset the deficit.

Piquet caught up eventually and made two attempts to get past into the first corner, one on the inside, one on the outside. The second manoeuvre stuck, and the irate Piquet then brake-tested his compatriot and waved his arm in protest even though he himself had made the pass into a right-hand corner with his steering wheel on left lock! This manoeuvre, the deadpan Clive

James commented, was completed with 'Piquet making the sign of the cross and Senna closing his eyes'.

Austria was a wasted race: Senna only qualified eighth and then retired with a dud engine on lap 13, but that was nothing compared to Monza, where he hit a piece of debris on the track during qualifying, which hurt his preparations – and then his transmission called it a day on the start grid. The Lotus crawled down to the first chicane while it was engulfed by the rest of the field in scenes uncomfortably reminiscent of the build-up to the accident eight years earlier that had claimed the life of Ronnie Peterson.

The season had not differed a great deal from 1985 at this point – two wins and several wasted opportunities, some through no fault of his own – but Senna was still in with a mathematical chance of the title. In Portugal Bernie Ecclestone arranged the famous photocall in which Senna, Prost, Mansell and Piquet, the four title protagonists, posed on the pit wall with their arms around each other. Of the two in the picture, an unnamed driver revealed that only Prost and Mansell got on with each other at this stage, and even that wouldn't last following their tenure at Ferrari four years later. It is well known that there are few genuine friendships in Formula 1.

As is always the way, at the race in which Senna was photographed as a candidate for the title he dropped out of a contention, cruelly robbed of second place in the dying stages as his fuel read-out was telling him fibs.

Nigel Roebuck was fulsome in his praise of Senna's effortless passage through lapped traffic – describing his approach as 'mesmeric, blending sublime judgment and tremendous courage time and again' – something for which he would remain famous for the remainder of his career.

At the first Mexican Grand Prix for sixteen years Senna was again on the pole, although as was his wont he was actually annoyed because he had hit a bump and had to back off, reckoning he could have gone half a second quicker!

There were some rivals who were now openly suspecting that the team was cheating, murmuring amongst themselves that the amount of sparks that appeared from Senna's car on Fridays and Saturdays may have indicated an illegally flexing floor. Lotus took a dim view of this criticism and set out an irate press release to quell the whispers. Gerard Ducarouge said bluntly that the times were the result of Senna, not the car.

Although teammate Johnny Dumfries did not have the advantage of the latest evolutions of equipment, he was nevertheless 3.489 seconds and sixteen grid positions behind Senna. Ducarouge had a point.

The Australian Grand Prix is regarded as one of the most dramatic races in the history of Grand Prix racing – and for good reason. Unfortunately, despite rivals' assertions that Senna would want to win simply to deny Piquet the title, he was never part of the drama and retired with engine failure after a dispiritingly quiet afternoon.

Meanwhile, Nigel Mansell's left rear tyre exploded as he was en route to the safe third place that would have netted him his first crown and Alain Prost, having looked to be out of contention after an early puncture, was there to pick up the spoils. It was cruel luck for Mansell, to say the least. His manhandling of the bucking three-wheeled car into the escape road without being seriously injured was one of the most definitive pieces of car control ever exhibited in a Formula 1 car. Alain Prost, however, thoroughly deserved his victory.

Senna had again finished fourth in the standings – a reflection of his car's thirst and unreliability rather than any personal failing, bar a couple of below-par races. He had improved his points tally immeasurably, though, from 38 to 55, and must have hoped this pattern would continue.

In November, after the season had finished, Senna gave his JPS overalls one last day out in the forests of Wales.

He had been persuaded by his friend, the late motoring writer Russell Bulgin, to travel to the mountains to try out a selection of rally cars – MG Metro 6R4, Vauxhall Nova, Ford Sierra, Ford Escort and VW Golf – for Bulgin's magazine *Cars and Car Conversions*, no household publication but one which nevertheless had itself a rather sizeable scoop.

One of Senna's guides for the day was Phil Collins – not the balding drummer whose records Senna enjoyed on a regular basis – but the Herefordshire-based rally driver. After his first run in the co-driver's seat, Senna leaped out and shouted 'Too quick for me! He's a nut-case!'

'It's a pity it's so rough out there or I could really scare the little b*****d', was the dry reply.

However, despite Collins' best attempts to further undermine his confidence by pointing out the position of reverse gear 'for reversing back out of those trees', Senna quickly learned the ropes when behind the steering wheel.

'You can see the talent of the guy within two-and-a-half miles,' Collins said. 'He made a right balls of the first corner, but you could feel the embarrassment. By the time we did the second run the guy was driving with a lot of confidence.'

Allan Edwards, the builder of the Escort, concluded: 'In a matter of hours he [Senna] would be a national class forest driver and I would say after a week in a car he would be taking on the world class drivers.'

Notwithstanding the occasional white-knuckle moment, Senna thoroughly enjoyed himself, even offering to build Collins a passenger seat in his Lotus and return the favour. Indeed, Senna called it his best ever day in England (even though he was in Wales).

Bulgin's report of the session ends 'In a cafe at the entrance to the stage, over soup and a cream-cake, Ayrton Senna attempts to rationalise rallying. He looks happy, relaxed, a thousand miles away from the niggles of Formula 1.'

1987: The Rising Son

For 1987 Lotus stole a major march on Williams by gaining a Honda power supply of their own, following Renault's complete withdrawal after a year as just an engine supplier. The stiff–upper-lipped Dumfries returned to his country estate to make way for Satoru Nakajima, a Japanese driver to whom Lotus were obliged to give their second seat under the terms of their new Honda contract. Although handy in the wet, Nakajima's deficit to his new teammate in qualifying was often to the tune of around four whole seconds, so for the second season running Senna had things his way.

This was the start of a special relationship between Senna and the Japanese manufacturer which would last until 1992.

In Belgium he ran foul yet again of Nigel Mansell. Senna qualified third behind the Williams cars but at the second start (the first attempt was aborted after a crash) he leaped into the lead but soon had the superior car of the Brit swarming all over him as the pair headed into the Les Fagnes corner. Senna stayed right, on the inside lane, and Mansell dived to the outside and attempted a pass. With only one camera angle of the incident available, it was difficult to apportion blame, although both commentator James Hunt and Mansell himself were in no doubt.

Senna was out on the spot, and Mansell retired after trundling round with accident damage for a further seventeen laps. En route to his dressing room he called into the Lotus garage and grabbed the Brazilian round the neck, zipping his overalls up to his nose in a scene that probably would have been rather comic despite the circumstances. Senna also demonstrated an aptitude for rather dry wit when he was asked what the burly Englishman had come to say to him.

'When a man holds you round the throat, I do not think he has come to apologise.'

In Mexico Senna let his temper, a beast never too difficult to awaken, get the better of him. After spinning off he took a leaf out of James Hunt's book and decked one of the marshals, for which he was fined $15,000. One wonders how much of this, if any, went to the marshal himself.

The aspect over which he exercised no real control was the chassis. The new 99T was heavily compromised by Ducarouge's decision to incorporate complicated active suspension technology, which would become *de rigeur* in later seasons but in 1987 was still in its infancy. The car with the arresting new Camel yellow livery was yet again only good for two wins, but one of these was the first of Senna's incredible six victories around the streets of Monte Carlo after polesitter Nigel Mansell lost an eleven-second lead with turbo failure.

After the race he was collared by the local *gendarmerie* for riding on the back of a friend's motorcycle as he made his way to a late-night hotspot to celebrate his victory, but was soon released after they realised who he was.

The other was a repeat victory in Detroit which, although nobody knew it then, was to date the 73rd and last victory for the great Team Lotus.

At Monza, Senna worked miracles to keep the much faster Piquet behind him on ancient tyres that were many laps overdue for a change. Eventually he pressure got too much and he ran wide at Parabolica, but even so he set the race's fastest lap as he recovered to finish only a second behind his compatriot.

Now 27, Senna may have been feeling that he was squandering his unparalleled talent with a team that seemed to be springing more holes than repairing leaks. The 99T was a rather ungainly creature: in fact the legend 'Camel' on the bodywork seemed rather apt. In comparison to the sleek, cigar-tube-shaped Types 25, 33 and 49 it didn't seem quite worthy of the Lotus name, somehow.

To add insult to injury he was denied second place in the world championship for the most trifling of oversights at the Australian Grand Prix. After he had obliged Glen Dix, the enthusiastic yellow-coated waver of the chequered flag, to almost bury himself in the pit wall as he roared past, scrutineers found the brake ducts of Senna's second-placed car to be of illegal dimensions and disqualified him. This meant that he failed to overhaul the absent Nigel Mansell, who had been denied a crack at the title for the second year running by a crash in practice at Suzuka, which had eliminated him from contention in the final two races of the season.

Alain Prost, who had also been reduced to a supporting role by the Williams-Hondas' dominance, finished the year a quiet fourth despite becoming Formula 1's most successful driver in terms of race victories at Estoril. It was the first time since 1982 that Prost had not been a serious challenger for the championship.

The fortunes of both Prost and Senna would change dramatically the following year.

7

A Prosty Relationship

No biography of Ayrton Senna could leave the printing press without mention of his relationship with Alain Prost. Without the other, it is unlikely either would have achieved the status they have.

The received wisdom is that Senna wanted to destroy Prost – not just metaphorically, but literally. Prost says it himself. His crime? To be too good.

In an assessment of Senna's career it is arguable that he should have hated other rivals far more than he did the little Frenchman. Recall Nelson Piquet said that Senna was gay as well as unceremoniously comparing him to a 'taxi driver'; Nigel Mansell crashed into Senna on at least five prominent occasions, and Michael Schumacher essentially told the press that he thought Senna was a dirty driver (which was perhaps a bit rich).

Before the start of the 1987 season there had been surprisingly prescient rumours about Senna joining Prost at McLaren-Honda, but all the chatter proved to have foundation.

McLaren had been in steady if slow decline since their dominance of 1984, and 1987's MP4/3, unlike its two predecessors, was retired after just one season. The TAG Porsche turbo, one of the secret ingredients in the rejuvenated team three years previously, was now outclassed by the might of Honda, and Ron Dennis knew he had to get in on the action if he was to take the fight to Frank Williams's cars.

Williams's new world champion Nelson Piquet had decided that life at Grove wasn't what he had been expecting. Despite having everything from the first pick of new parts to first dibs on the team Portaloo, the Brazilian was somewhat chagrined that these privileges did not extend to the track. Nigel Mansell's refusal to lie prone in the road and capitulate to his elder colleague continued to displease Piquet immensely.

Meanwhile, Senna was also casting his net. After three seasons with Lotus his career had plateaued, with two wins every year being an inaccurate reflection of his capabilities. Then as now, Formula 1 drivers can have the talent of an entire symphony orchestra but if they find themselves in less than optimal machinery they will fail to chalk up the hard statistics with which so many are fixated and by which ultimate status is determined.

Senna was rather clandestine in his assessment of new employers, and when Peter Warr got wind of his star driver's roving eye, he swiftly swept both Piquet from Williams to partner Nakajima for 1988, and the rug from under Senna's feet.

Senna was far from impressed, feeling that Warr had made him look like a fool.

'It amazes me that a company as big and famous as Lotus should behave so unprofessionally. They could have called me the day he signed to let me know, but instead I found out on Friday morning.'

This was blisteringly hypocritical stuff, given Senna's defection from the Toleman team three years before; what he expected from those around him did not necessarily have to be doled out with a generous hand in return.

Retrospectively it is easy to wonder what Warr was putting in his tea, letting a driver as fast and hungry as Senna go in exchange for a man who would not lift one victory for the team in his two years there. But it is worth remembering that at the time, Piquet was a newly crowned triple champion and Senna was an occasional winner.

Over at McLaren, there was a vacancy. Swede Stefan Johansson was only ever a stopgap driver after Keke Rosberg's retirement at the end of 1986 and had put in a workmanlike 1987 season. He failed to win any races for the Woking squad and his most noteworthy escapade involved hitting a deer at the Osterreichring and narrowly avoiding being vaporised.

Prost wanted a young, ambitious driver to partner him. Ron Dennis, swayed by Senna's speed, commitment and familiarity with Honda, didn't need asking twice.

Prost had a flavour of what Senna was like a few years earlier in 1984, when the two competed in a Mercedes touring car race to commemorate the opening of the new Nurburgring. Prost had been dispatched to collect Senna from the airport to take him there, and apparently the younger man was impressed by the speeds at which Prost hustled his car along the German roads. Their rapport remained until Prost beat his erstwhile passenger to pole position for the race. That was the end of the banter! (Senna, who was not even scheduled to race, then beat Prost and all the other established Grand Prix stars to the victory, so his petulance soon evaporated.)

Nevertheless, to begin with relations were as friendly as is possible when two Grand Prix drivers are striving to assert themselves in the same team. The announcement of Senna as Johannson's replacement, in the Monza forest in September 1987, is captured in the *Senna* film, and at that point there seemed to be nothing but cordiality and professional respect between the two men. Senna says, 'It's a great opportunity for me as a professional and from a personal point of view I am very happy to work with Alain: two top drivers working together can only make a team stronger.'

Derek Warwick could have been forgiven for choking on his coffee at that statement.

Prost's riposte: 'I know that Ayrton is very professional and I will help him integrate into the team ... but of course I will do my best to beat him on the track.'

Then there was the small matter of the new car.

McLaren's new drivers would find themselves armed with a piece of equipment that ensured they would have to fall asleep at the wheel to be anywhere near the rear of the field. From 1989 onwards the turbocharged engines that had caused so many safety concerns were to be replaced by a new formula for normally aspirated 3.5 litre units, and the '88 rules reduced the turbo boost from 4.0 to 2.5 bar in order to try and rein in some of the near suicidal power outputs previously seen.

Rather than scale back their efforts on the forced-induction V6, Honda came up with a brand new unit for '88, the RA168E, and the new MP4/4 made full use of it.

Designed by South African guru Gordon Murray and American Steve Nichols, the new car was visibly sleeker and slicker than anything that had gone before. It took the low-slung principle of Murray's Brabham BT55 from two years prior, but this time made it work. It was so close to the ground that Nichols was constantly telling his drivers to duck further into the cockpit to increase aerodynamic efficiency, as their crash helmets disturbed airflow if they sat too high. Even the previous year's MP4/3, on which the 4/4 was based, looked like a hippo in comparison. Despite only being ready at the eleventh hour for pre-season testing at Imola (during which Prost made a gallant and successful attempt at out-psyching Senna by not getting out of the only car available when it was Senna's turn to have a go) it was a pace-setter straight out of the box, and what a pace it was.

Battle commenced in Brazil, where Prost had won four times. Despite Senna starting on pole, Prost cruised to his fifth success in Rio as Senna struggled with his gear selector on the parade lap and was then disqualified for changing to the spare McLaren after the green flag had been shown. Senna had been mighty up to that point, climbing all the way from last place to second behind Prost by lap 20, but his efforts were to be in vain.

Imola was the first of ten one-two finishes, with Senna recording his first win at the track that would carry such tragic resonance exactly six years to the day. The pace was so explosive that Senna and Prost both lapped faster in race trim than Lotus's Nelson Piquet, with the same engine, had managed in qualifying the day before! Even more incredibly, the qualifying time in question had put Piquet third on the grid. That is a measure of how superior McLaren's new car was. It was 1984 all over again, and then some. Up and down the pit lane rang the sound of engineers' heads being banged off brick walls.

Round three was at Monaco, and this became one of the most famous races in the sport's history for two reasons, both of them involving Senna.

If anyone had ever doubted Senna's incredible talent before qualifying in Monte Carlo, the results were there for all to see. Senna finished Saturday's session 1.427 seconds faster than Alain Prost – himself a holder of 16 pole positions up to that point – who was second on the grid!

Later he gave the now famous interview to Canadian journalist Gerald Donaldson, in which he described the otherworldly sensation he felt during the session, another well-worn part of Senna folklore – but for a good reason.

Donaldson says: 'He was the most thoughtful, introspective, articulate – even in his second language, English – of any driver I have ever spoken to. Plus he had a magnetic personality. All of those things. You got so much material from him, he worked so hard at it. If you interviewed him, he would be focusing so intently, it was sometimes kind of frightening ... one on one with him, or even in a media centre with 100 people there.'

Senna was not the first driver to annihilate a teammate in qualifying, but he was the first to go into the psychological and philosophical reasons of how he did it.

For all the mystical awe his very sincere account eluded, the second reason the race is remembered was due to an altogether more earthly concept: human error. On Sunday Senna was so far ahead of Prost, as was expected of him given his clear speed superiority, that the Frenchman may as well have been in Italy. Senna decided to back off. Prost had been plugged behind Berger's Ferrari and, when he eventually got past, reminded both the watching world and his teammate that he wasn't quite as useless as they all seemed to be thinking. He was, after all, a winner of this race on three occasions.

He started to close the gap, as difficult an exercise as this may have been, and in one lap alone chopped six seconds off Senna's lead. Spooked, Senna quickened his pace and upon entering Portier for the 67th time he clipped the inside barrier and was spat across the track into the other piece of Armco. That colossal qualifying advantage over Prost had been negated in a moment of poor judgment. Senna got out, removed his helmet and walked away, apparently calm. It was only later, when he got home, that the tears would start. Prost streaked past to Monte Carlo win number four in five years. He had thrown away an easy win in the Principality six years earlier, and now fortune smiled on him.

Senna's explanation for his exit again touched on more meta-physical themes than simply driving into a wall under pressure and were, ironic as the term is, manna from heaven for the hordes of cynical journalists.

In wake of the accident, Senna told Mike Doodson that he crashed because he had slowed down and lost concentration, which didn't tally with what McLaren told everyone: namely that he ... well, hadn't. When Doodson put it to him that there was a spiritual element to the crash, he told him, with admirable brevity, to 'f*ck off.' But at least he admitted he made a mistake.

Yet he later told *Playboy* that yes, there *had* been a light, shining out at sea, ordering him to sacrifice the race. When Doodson drew attention to this apparent *volte-face*, Senna refused to speak to him again.

Prost continued his run of successes in Mexico, winning and setting fastest lap, while polesitter Senna was stymied by an issue with his turbo's pop-off valve. In Canada things were close with Prost qualifying only a tenth behind Senna and leading for the first part of the race, before Senna managed to sneak past and win by six seconds.

This display of brilliance by the red and white cars was not appreciated by all onlookers, however.

'In our innocence, we thought we might get a race this time. Oh, if someone else could lead just a lap, what bliss it would be …' was how *Autosport's* race report from Canada that year began.

Some call it boring, while others are happy to be witnessing giants of the sport create history.

When Ron Dennis was accused by sections of the press of having a McLaren team that was too good, Frank Williams apparently defended him claiming it was his responsibility, and that of the competing teams, to be competitive and do the job for which they were all paid so handsomely.

Senna had been the winner in Detroit for the past two years and he made it a hat trick in 1988. Prost openly admitted he couldn't live with his teammate: an open opponent of the Michigan street circuit, he finished nearly 40 seconds behind.

'I had to change my whole way of driving, brake carefully in a straight line, then turn in. No excuse, you understand, but it meant adapting, doing something which isn't my natural style.'

However, Alain didn't need to adapt to anything at the French Grand Prix – always peerless around Paul Ricard, he was superior to Senna all weekend and set pole for the first time that season. Even when he fell behind his teammate, Prost reeled him in and overtook him, setting fastest lap on the way to his third home win.

Silverstone saw Formula 1's first rain affected Grand Prix since Estoril three years earlier, where a certain yellow-helmeted chap in the number 12 car had won. Even though McLaren didn't get qualifying right, being beaten by Ferrari's Berger to pole, the situation wouldn't change.

'Race day though, was Senna-made. He might not care for slippery or perilous conditions any more than anyone else, but they are manna to him, bringing out all his artistry,' said *Autosport*'s race report once again.

Casual viewers may have been wondering who the strange man on the second step of the podium was: Mansell had shaved off his moustache.

Senna and Prost were on target to win every single race in 1988 until the Italian Grand Prix, where a mistake from Senna cost Ron Dennis his clean sweep. Nigel Mansell was laid low with chickenpox and his stand-in was a journeyman called Jean-Louis Schlesser, who would unwittingly become one of the sport's more famous one-off drivers when he and Senna tangled at the first chicane as the McLaren was trying to lap the Williams. The scarcely-believing Italians watched as their beloved Ferraris took the flag one-two in the first race at Monza since the death of *Commendatore* Enzo Ferrari just weeks before.

In the run up to the Portuguese race, Senna and Prost sat side by side in the press conference, lazing on leather recliners. Senna had an affectionate arm lopped behind Prost, like a protective boyfriend. Prost jokingly asked if it was possible for them both to be crowned world champion. 'No, there can only be one winner,' laughed Senna, although one got the impression he was deadly serious. Prost simply replied, 'Sh*t.'

Just in case Prost had got the wrong idea from this show of joviality, Senna reminded him of who he thought was boss by trying to drive him into the pit wall on lap 2. Although Prost gritted his teeth and kept his foot in to win the race, there was to be no more jostling.

'If we'd touched at that speed, it would have been like a plane crash. I knew Ayrton wanted the world championship, but it wasn't until today that I realised he was prepared to die for it. If he wants it that badly, he can have it ...'

And Senna did want it badly. When he was less angry Prost calmly conceded the title, saying that a man of the Brazilian's ability would make a worthy champion (although he would still have a crack at lifting it himself, of course).

The Frenchman was actually ahead on points but the scoring system at the time curiously only counted the best eleven results from sixteen rounds, or to put it another way, drivers dropped their five worst scores as the season reached its conclusion.

This takes a little explanation.

After the preceding round at Jerez, Prost was leading the title chase with 90 points in total and 84 counting. This means that he had been doing so well over the course of the season that one of his *worst* results was a second place, so he jettisoned six points. Senna, meanwhile, had won seven races to that point but when his races went badly he had fared much worse than Prost, which was paradoxically a blessing: those pointless finishes didn't affect his overall score at all. Prost could only gain meaningful points for the remaining two rounds by winning both of them: a second place was no good to him.

The system favoured Senna's all-out approach rather than Prost's point harvesting, something that Senna would draw attention to when he said that he had lost his respect for his teammate because he only knew how to drive for second places.

And so it came to pass at Suzuka that Senna could win the 1988 title by also winning the race, no calculations required, he just had to go for it. Even if Prost was to win the race after in Australia, it would only net him a paltry three points instead of the full nine.

Unfortunately at the start he stalled. As the field screamed past him with Prost untroubled in the lead, Senna kept his head. In the modern age he might have had anti-stall software to keep his chances alive: but all he needed back then was a little luck. The start at Suzuka is on a slight downward slope, so Senna disengaged the clutch, trickled forward, bump started and got going.

In fact, 'got going' is a rather pedestrian way of putting it: Senna knew that he could fulfil his boyhood dream that day and a minor inconvenience such as running in fourteenth place wasn't going to stop him.

By lap 2 he was up to eighth, by lap 4, fourth. And then the rain started to fall. Senna kept going faster and faster until he was on Prost's tail. And on lap 14, as Prost was stymied by traffic, Senna rocketed past him and into the lead, from which he was not separated again. He had done it: he was the world champion. And, according to Senna, it wasn't just the Japanese fans he saw on the slowing-down lap, but God as well.

After the race, Senna's good friend and Brazilian broadcaster Reginaldo Leme said to him that he had often been ruthless and had pushed people aside, so would he remember the people who helped him reach the top? The interviewee burst into tears, in a characteristic open display of emotion.

1989: Sabotage at Suzuka

Senna and Prost were still on speaking terms, and remained very much the title favourites for 1989. It would have needed a serious decline in fortune for anyone other than one of the two of them to be world champion again in the final year of the decade.

The Brazilian Grand Prix provided something of a false dawn as Ferrari won with Nigel Mansell first time out. This was a surprise to everyone, none more so than the man himself, who had booked himself an early plane home as he didn't think the car would be able to leave the pitlane without spluttering to a halt. Senna clashed with Gerhard Berger in an accident that looked similar to what would happen at Suzuka the following year.

Still, he had only to wait until Round 2 at Imola for his first victory of the season; McLaren having conducted a very thorough test there to make sure they were not beaten again.

The race began in dramatic fashion. Rounding Tamburello, Berger's Ferrari suffered a mechanical failure and speared into a giant billboard (ironically, for team fuel supplier Agip's Emichem brand) at unabated speed. Within seconds the 640 burst into flames with the unconscious Berger still inside. To their credit the fire marshals were quickly on the scene and doused the flames, and their swift action along with the strength of the carbon fibre monocoque and Berger's fireproof overalls meant the Austrian was largely unhurt, suffering only burns to his hands and broken ribs.

Shrugging off the severity of the accident, he made light of being knocked unconscious by the impact, chuckling, 'I sleep a little bit because I was tired.'

He would miss only one race. Like his compatriot and Ferrari predecessor before him, Niki Lauda, he didn't let the little matter of being involved in a huge fiery crash throw him off his stride. Hardy souls, these Austrians.

Mercifully the story of Berger post-accident was a happy one, but that crash would have a further-reaching effect than was at first obvious. Unfortunately, the reprofiling of the corner was not one of them.

Some time later, Berger walked around Imola with Senna. Both agreed the demon Tamburello turn was dangerous, and yet both concurred that there was not much that could be done since a river ran behind the perimeter wall. Sadly, it would take the events of 1994 to illustrate something could indeed have been changed.

But that was in the future. Berger's accident had brought out the red flags and after he had been taken to hospital and the debris cleared away, the field lined up on the grid once more.

As Prost and Senna, inevitably at the head of the field, swept through Villeneuve and into Tosa, Senna lined up Prost and glided past. To the outside world, this looked fair enough, as he was clearly quicker, further emphasized by Senna's eventual forty second winning margin, but Prost was raging and refused to attend the post-race press conference.

It emerged Senna had, by passing him into Tosa, breached an agreement not to pass into the first braking zone – an agreement Prost claimed was Senna's idea! Senna was unrepentant: he retorted there had been a verbal understanding that the man behind would not sling one up the inside into the corner, but it had only applied to the first, invalidated, start.

This cut no mustard with Prost who was so incensed he told Ron Dennis he was on the verge of quitting the team as he could not work in an atmosphere of such treachery. Dennis, not keen on the idea of losing one of his star drivers and a major draw for what he would call his 'corporate partners,' went into PR overdrive and did his best to smooth over the cracks after the matter. This came to a head at a test at Pembrey in Wales the following week. Dennis making Senna apologise for breaching the agreement, although Senna got so wound up over this that he cried, which gives an indication of how correct he believed he had been and the hurt he felt when his beliefs were challenged.

His counter-argument was rather compelling: 'He [Prost] lost fair and square. Even if he had led at the first bend, I would have beaten him. I was faster that day, that's all. What was I supposed to do? Lift my foot off the accelerator on the straight because I was going faster than him? Are we racing or aren't we?'

Meantime, Prost, in a decision he now deeply regrets, vented his disgust to a *L'Equipe* journalist who he considered to be a friend on the condition that his sniping remained private. His friend skipped off and published the comments, having evidently misunderstood, or chosen to ignore the meaning of 'off' in 'off the record.'

Senna was appalled by the Frenchman's behaviour, and there was to be no reconciliation this time – the younger man vowed that as far as niceties were concerned, he and Prost were finished.

Over the course of the season Senna continued to demonstrate what he did best. His pace was arguably even more scorching than the previous year and Prost could very rarely get anywhere near to him in a straight fight. The only time that Alain was genuinely ahead in all respects was, as ever, on home ground in France.

Although Senna's reliability was incomparably worse than his teammate's with wins in San Marino, Monaco and Mexico it would have seemed incredible at this stage to suggest that he would not win the world championship in 1989. Even Prost's fans would have admitted that the Professor was looking a little pedestrian, having never overtaken Senna in the heat of competition.

However, momentum can swing very quickly in Formula 1, as Prost himself knew well. The summer saw a run of four races in which Senna failed to finish on the podium or even the points, handing the advantage back to Prost.

In qualifying for the US Grand Prix at the angular new Phoenix street circuit, Senna notched up his 34th pole position, beating the record held by his childhood hero Jim Clark, which clearly meant a lot to him, but the rot for Senna began to set in. His Honda engine gave up, his first failure with a Japanese powerplant in 37 races, and Prost won. As if to make up for lost time, his engine let go again in Canada, although polesitter Prost also trundled off with broken suspension.

In France, Senna's engine held together but his differential barely got the MP4/5 off the line. This occurred at a restart, triggered by Senna's over-exuberant chum Mauricio Gugelmin arriving at the first corner upside down first time round. Prost, who had taken his second and last pole position of the year, won his home race at Paul Ricard as per normal and repeated the feat a week later at Silverstone. This time he was helped by Senna, struggling with the McLaren's new gearbox layout, putting a wheel wide at Becketts and spinning out of the lead.

It was at Silverstone that it was announced that Prost would be switching to Ferrari for the 1990 season, ending the fractious pairing with his intransigent Brazilian teammate, whom he suspected of somehow gleaning an unfair advantage.

Whether Senna was actually the recipient of better equipment is open to question, although McLaren always insisted that their drivers had total parity across the board. The advantage that Senna *did* have, for sure, was psychological. Much as he had done with de Angelis at Lotus four years before, he had arrived at a team with an incumbent star driver and wasted no time bending them to his will. Prost may have been with McLaren for seven seasons (including his single pre-Ron Dennis year in 1980) but that didn't stop him feeling very uncomfortable.

Of course this happens in racing all the time. It is inherently a selfish sport which drives individuals to seek personal success. Prost, despite his accusations, was then blasted by Nigel Mansell the next year for allegedly doing the same thing at Ferrari. There is no such thing in the modern age as a successful racing driver who isn't as adept at manoeuvering off the track as well as he is on it. The last breed of drivers to truly believe in sportsmanship and fairness of competition wore flat caps and addressed each other as 'old chap'.

In later years this even happened to Senna himself. By the 1993 season, his criticism of the team, open desire to join Williams and prohibitive wage demands had made him the cuckoo in McLaren's nest and Ron Dennis was openly quite fond of the team's new charger, Mika Hakkinen, who was seen as the team's future.

Germany saw yet more McLaren success, but unlike the previous handful of events there was a genuine head-to-head between the two drivers. A litany of errors by the pit crew hampered both drivers and for a time it was anybody's guess as to who would finish ahead, but Senna prevailed and took his first win since Mexico over two months previously. But his run of retirements had seriously hampered his championship chances and the methodical Prost was now 17 points ahead. With today's inflated scoring system this deficit could virtually be overcome merely by showing up to the race, but in 1989 it would be a tougher job for the Brazilian to carry the number 1 again in 1990.

Senna was uncharacteristically cautious in traffic in Hungary and got himself trapped behind Stefan Johansson's Onyx, allowing the Ferrari of Nigel Mansell to take his most memorable win. Prost had a lacklustre race, commenting that he felt 'more and more alone in the team'.

In Belgium, Senna was the only driver in serious contention for victory at Spa, dominating the wet race from the start to record his third win at the Wallonian circuit in soaking conditions. Prost finished a solid second, playing his usual percentage game, but took the victory next time out at Monza when Senna's engine blew. As the Brazilian's McLaren spun to a smoking halt at Parabolica, the sportsmanlike Italian crowd roared their approval as his elimination elevated their new French hero to the top step.

Prost's win was especially sweet for him given that he now felt utterly alienated by almost everybody at McLaren. In qualifying he had been 1.790 seconds behind Senna and had said, agape: 'Ayrton was very difficult to beat in qualifying … but I could not accept I was that much slower.'

Knowing that his bridges with McLaren were smoking already, Prost stoked the flames further by dropping his winner's trophy into the sea of adoring *tifosi* below the podium. Ron Dennis, whose drivers are contractually obliged to donate their silverware to McLaren, was appalled at being deprived of a piece for his bulging cabinet and threw his own Constructors' trophy at his errant driver's feet. Prost cared little: 'When I was on the podium I was more a Ferrari driver than a McLaren one. So I threw the cup to them – not on purpose to get at Ron. I am very much more natural than people think.'

Jo Ramirez, one of the few team members who remained on good terms with both sides of the garage, said: 'Prost – one of the greatest drivers we have ever seen – was never going to be almost two seconds slower than Senna. That weekend was ugly.'

Following a bad-tempered tangle with Mansell in Portugal, which led the melodramatic Brit to threaten retirement, a second title for Senna now looked like a fantasy. Senna needed to win at Jerez to keep his fading hopes alive but win he did, after a processional race to the flag. The stage was set for a title show-down at Suzuka.

The 1989 Japanese Grand Prix is one of the most famous, and infamous, races in motorsport history. By the time the circus reached Suzuka Alain Prost was now openly questioning the parity of the engines with which he and Senna were being supplied. To many this sounded like sour grapes. Prost was never a man to withhold his excuses for a poor performance, after all, and it seemed that he was simply scrabbling for justification after a second season of being outpaced, if not outscored, by his junior colleague. Yet one could see where he was coming from.

Martin Brundle says: 'Honda would build Senna an engine for qualifying ... they just knew that Senna could make the most of it. I don't think they felt that about Prost.'

Senna had worked with Honda at Lotus in 1987 and also spoke some Japanese. He was worshipped by the Japanese public in a way that Prost was not and was heavily involved with the development of the NSX road car.

Prost was yet again country miles behind Senna in practice and was starting to treat it as a bit of an unfunny joke.

Even the year before, Prost had started to mutter darkly that the McLaren concept of apparent equality didn't seem to have made it over the Pacific to Japan, so much so that Honda F1 boss Nobohiku Kawamoto arranged dinner with him to apologise, allegedly admitting that his engineers preferred Senna's 'samurai' nature.

Prost was convinced there was a conspiracy:

> In France, Senna never beat me in qualifying, so maybe
> you have an explanation for that?

> Let me give you an example. At one point in '88, the last
> year we were allowed to run turbos, I asked for some
> specific changes to the engine to suit my driving style and
> we worked on it for two days at Paul Ricard. At the end
> of that test I was very happy – but at the next race, one
> week later, they never put that strategy on my engine.
> Then we went to the French Grand Prix – at Ricard –
> and suddenly the engine was just as I had wanted! You
> understand what I'm saying?

This led Ron Dennis to categorically state that his team would
never deviate from its mission to ensure complete parity between
its drivers. 'Through their periods at McLaren, they always had
equality,' he later said. 'We would go to quite extreme lengths.
Engine choice, for example: it would be a number out of a hat
routine. This was trying to eliminate the view that Honda was
selecting what engines went to whom. But there was a degree of
paranoia because it didn't need much to determine who won the
race and who became world champion.'

A cynic would challenge this assertion on the basis that the
relationship between Senna and both Dennis and Honda was, at
this stage, light years ahead of that between Honda and Prost.
Alain could hardly complain: he had started to quite openly voice
his opinions on Senna and Dennis to the press. And he wasn't
saying what top blokes he thought they were.

'Ron was behind Ayrton but I understood that quickly. It's a
business. Ayrton was the new generation.'

In the title chase Prost was 16 points ahead of Senna but
thanks to the 'dropped scores' system that had caused him such

chagrin the previous year, Senna could still win the title if he won the remaining two races. This was unquestionably possible for the man whose reputation was that of a winner. He needed to dominate the Japanese Grand Prix.

At the start, however, Prost forgot that his engine was supposed to be inferior and rocketed off into the lead in a manner on which Senna had had the copyright most of the year. His first lap was a second and a half quicker than Ayrton's. He had opted for a different, low-downforce set-up from Senna, which made his MP4–5 like a greased eel down the straights but less sure of itself in the twisty bits, where the predatory Senna would reel him in again.

'All I can do today,' Prost said on the morning of the race, 'is attack, attack, attack. There's nothing else for it: Senna has to win to keep a chance of the championship, and the best way to stop him is to beat him.'

'It was very clear that I was quicker,' he said many years on. 'And, believe me or not, but I was playing with him. I was really fast. I said to Ron and Ayrton two or three races before, because every time Ayrton tried to overtake at the start I always opened the door because I don't want a crash, "From now, there is no way I will open the door any more. Don't care about team spirit, I fight for myself".'

At one stage the gap between the McLarens was six seconds and it looked as though, despite his self-imposed underdog status, Prost had risen to the challenge and thrown his usual softly, softly approach to the winds. Although his crash helmet obscured his face, there can be no doubt that his jaw was clenched. But, as Murray Walker always reminded us, anything can happen in Formula 1. Especially when Ayrton Senna was involved.

Senna closed inexorably on the Frenchman, seemingly running on pure adrenaline, until the gap between them was only a second. After a few laps where he was just out of reach, he dived down the inside of Prost in an opportunistic lunge as they entered the chicane for the forty-sixth time.

What happened next will remain a topic of Formula 1 debate for many decades to come.

After the searing pace of the gladiatorial contest between them, it was incongruously pathetic for the showdown to end with the two McLarens locking together at no more than a snail's pace and slithering down the escape road. The fight was over. Prost looked across at Senna and waved a hand like an exasperated parent, while Senna held his head in despair. Prost leaped out of the car so quickly it was almost as if he had been expecting to be taken out. When he later spoke on the subject, it became apparent that he had.

'And somehow I always thought the race would be decided one of two ways; either he would lead from the start, or it would finish like this. I looked in my mirrors, saw where he was, and thought he was too far back to try anything – he had been closer than that before, and stayed behind. Then he came down the inside.'

And then some words Senna's rivals in every formula had uttered since 1973:

'You know Ayrton's problem? He can't accept not winning, and because of that he can't accept someone resisting his overtaking manoeuvres – too many times he tries to intimidate people out of his way.'

Prost was seemingly the 1989 champion, although his body language suggested that he wasn't overjoyed about it.

'Ron Dennis showed us the helicopter shots taken above the chicane and it's quite clear that when they were both going into the chicane side by side, which is ludicrous, that Prost turned into Senna,' says Mike Doodson. 'There's no question about that – he couldn't deny it.'

Prost didn't deny that it happened, but neither did he accept that he had done it on purpose:

'I promise you I did not [cause the crash] on purpose, but I did not open the door. It is very very different. If you are not a racing driver, at this corner, knowing the track and knowing this chicane, you cannot judge. It is a waste of time.'

Ron Dennis didn't agree with his driver: 'It was a bit less than not yielding. There was a level of aggression.'

Senna urged the marshals for a push start and he managed to bump the Honda back into life. With visible fury he wrestled the car around the bollards at the exit of the chicane and roared back to the pits, front wing drooping, for a new nose. Even after all the delays he was still only five seconds behind new leader Alessandro Nannini, and wasted no time catching and passing the Italian's Benetton at the same chicane as he had collided with Prost. The Italian looked like he was slightly surprised by the move, but there was no contact and Senna's path to victory was clear.

As he crossed the line, his delight was plain to see as he punched the sides of his crash helmet in disbelief. But his joy was short-lived: as he was mounting the steps to the podium, he was physically blocked by his old pal Jean-Marie Balestre.

He had been disqualified from the race. Not, as many would have imagined, for receiving a push start from the marshals, but for cutting the chicane. Senna would later admit that he felt he had been 'treated like a criminal' and even to the most disinterested observer his treatment appeared harsh. Ron Dennis opined that the application of the regulations was awry and his driver had been the victim of some draconian heavy-handedness. Some cynics pointed out that Senna had earlier escaped a race ban for ignoring black flags in Jerez, whereas Mansell had not in Portugal. It worked both ways.

Senna, for his part, was convinced that he had done nothing wrong. 'That was the only place I could overtake. And somebody who should not have been there just closed the door and that was that.'

Prost actually tried to shake his hand, to offer condolences for the loss of the title in this way, but Senna wasn't interested: indeed on top of his disqualification, he received a six-month suspended ban and was fined $100,000. McLaren found themselves at the FIA Court of Appeal in Paris in the extraordinary position of trying to defend one of the drivers to the detriment of the other. Prost was none too happy about this state of affairs, but McLaren's Creighton Brown insisted that the team were trying to reclaim the win they had lost to Nannini's Benetton.

When briefing the press afterwards, Ron Dennis's fury with the process was evident:'The appeal bore absolutely no semblance to the case we were fighting, several key issues were put forward. What we are fighting for is a consistent application of the regulations.'

The FIA clearly had an axe to grind with Senna and argued that the draconian punishment was merited on the basis of the Brazilian's numerous misdemeanours over the previous two seasons, causing jaws to drop at McLaren in utter disbelief.

The legitimacy of the whole operation was questioned by Dennis when he pointed out that some parts of the stewards' report had literally been Tipp-Exed over.

'I don't understand the reasoning,' said Frank Williams. 'To call Senna a dangerous driver is just ludicrous,' said Ken Tyrrell.

Senna himself was curiously quiet on the subject, but this did not mean that he was not profoundly affected by his treatment at the hands of the FIA. It had not escaped his notice that Prost, who enjoyed what he thought was an openly chummy relationship with fellow Frenchman Balestre, had been straight up to the stewards after the crash to protest against his race win, although Prost denies that it was that simple.

He had himself had been involved in a couple of run-ins with Balestre in the past, notably at Monza in 1986 when he was disqualified from the race, but Senna would not have cared.

'Ayrton was convinced that there was a conspiracy and the story started like this,' says Prost. 'I'm very sorry about that. Ron was already in the tower [race control]. I was never in the tower with Mr Balestre alone. I read that many times, it did not happen. I did not go into the race control.'

Senna had lost the title, his arguable superiority over Prost notwithstanding, at the same venue where the year before he said he had seen God as he rounded his first warm-down lap as world champion. In his darkest hour in Formula 1 yet, he must have once again looked to higher places for inner resolve.

In the great Senna/Prost war, Senna is often painted as the aggressor, and rightly so. But it is irrefutable that his treatment by the powers-that-be after Suzuka was verging on the ridiculous.

The title decided, the controversy rampant, Adelaide was a damp affair in more ways than one. Rain drenched the south Australian street circuit and Prost, title secured, ended his illustrious McLaren career by pulling into the pits at the end of lap one and saying he was damned if he was driving in those levels of visibility. Senna unintentionally underlined his point by driving full pelt into the back of Martin Brundle's unsighted Brabham, reducing the McLaren to a tricycle and invoking the Englishman's fury.

In spite of thirteen pole positions and six victories, 1989 had just not been Senna's year.

1990: Jeopardy in Japan

Ayrton Senna was the type of chap who didn't often regret making his feelings known: he usually had some degree of justification. But after the tumultuous events of the previous year he may have wished he had kept his opinions to himself.

So disgusted was he with his treatment at the hands of FISA that he told the press the events leading to the outcome of the world championship had been manipulation.

Jean-Marie Balestre, not renowned for his rational approach to such matters, went berserk. He announced that if the Brazilian thought his 1990 superlicense was in the post, he had another think coming. He was also incensed that the $100,000 fine imposed on the miscreant driver had not yet left the Brazilian's bank account.

At the last minute, Senna offered a harrumphing apology, although he obviously didn't mean it, and McLaren dug into the team coffers to pay the fine. Senna arrived in Phoenix a determined but rather disillusioned man.

One thing I have got very clear in my mind is that now I want to be in Phoenix, to be racing there, to race the whole championship,' he told the BBC's Steve Rider:

> I want to fight it right from beginning to end, to the best of my ability. And give a very good shot to get my second world title. Everything else is past – has not been forgotten – it is past, but I hope to use it as a good experience in order to prevent it happening again in the future.

> I don't regret anything. I just feel that I am doing things for the right reasons, some understand, some don't. You will never get everybody to agree and accept. Most of them admire, after all, what I'm doing as a professional, as a man, as many drivers do.

One parameter that may have cheered Senna in the midst of the pre-season politics was that he had a new teammate. In the three seasons that followed, Gerhard Berger and Senna would become more than teammates: their practical joking would become the bane of each other's lives and, on occasion, that of their team boss Ron Dennis.

There was a slight surprise in their first outing together when Berger beat Senna to provisional pole and then stayed there when the rain, an infrequent visitor to Arizona, paid a visit on Saturday. Thus Berger had stolen a march on his new cohort – he later admitted at the time he had jokily scoffed: 'Ayrton Senna? No problem!'

Having started only fifth, Senna soon found himself hounding Jean Alesi's Pirelli–shod Tyrrell, which qualified ahead of him. As they pounded towards the first corner, Senna slipstreamed the French-Sicilian's car and overtook him for the lead with a textbook outbraking manoeuvre.

Alesi, having presumably not been briefed about F1 protocol, promptly overtook the McLaren again at the next corner. Senna had evidently assumed the move was a done deal and hadn't even closed the door. The next time round, Senna made the move stick, but he was hounded by Alesi relentlessly for the rest of the lap and managed to extend a gap until the chequered flag fell.

In the press conference he smiled, obviously relieved that after the maelstrom of controversy at the end of the previous year he had started the new season with a little fun.

'It was a good fight, a clean fight, and these are the moments where I get enjoyment from my profession.'

He was also fulsome in his praise of the young Tyrrell driver. 'I personally admire him and I think that he has the hot blood that this sport needs. He has already demonstrated that he has bravery, talent and the class that is needed to achieve success.'

Unusually the season hadn't started in Brazil, it was instead the second race on the calendar. By now Senna's dearth of victories in his homeland was a bewildering anomaly in an otherwise excellent record, but a change of venue represented a fresh opportunity.

Interlagos (where the then Ayrton da Silva had met another one of his heroes, Emerson Fittipaldi, as a local schoolboy) had returned to the F1 stage in a new and abridged form.

Senna took pole but was hesitant through the backmarkers, being deprived of his front wing by former teammate Satoru Nakajima after the Tyrrell cut in front of him and being demoted to third. Like Rubens Barrichello years later, he seemed to be displaying an aversion to winning his home race. He smiled on the podium as he was commiserated by new Brazilian president Fernando Collor de Mello, but he had been beaten yet again by Prost, who was unable to contain his emotions at winning only his second race for the Scuderia. Prost had now taken a record six Brazilian Grand Prix victories while Senna still had none.

Imola saw a rare retirement for Senna, when he was forced into the gravel with a cracked wheel rim. The vociferous Italian crowd was rather particular about which drivers they deemed worthy guardians of the number 27 and the McLaren driver was not one of them. Senna gave his best show of implacability as he inspected the offending wheel, ignoring the boos and catcalls coming from the stands before kicking out at the tyres. For all the love that would later be directed his way due to events at the very same track, it was in short supply here.

Riccardo Patrese, meanwhile, took his first win for an unbelievable seven years. He wasn't a Ferrari driver but the spectators knew the significance and were polite enough to at least pretend to be happy for their countryman.

Monaco saw Senna's third win on the streets, from pole position, and he won again in Canada two weeks later after Berger was penalised for a jump start.

Prost had been somewhat anonymous for the past few races, and when he was left in thirteenth position after qualifying for Mexico it didn't seem likely the situation would change. Come race day, however, he put in a storming performance and, through a combination of his own blistering pace and the misfortune of others, took the win to close the gap to Senna in the title chase. Senna himself gambled on driving the whole race without a stop for fresh Goodyears, but this decision backfired as a tyre failure put him out with six laps to go.

It had been a low-key 100th Grand Prix for Ayrton, who only qualified in third the day before, but there was excitement aplenty in the latter stages as Mansell steeled himself and blasted around the outside of Gerhard Berger on the banked Peraltada corner in one of the most stunningly audacious (or worryingly stupid, according to the man himself) manoeuvres witnessed in modern Grand Prix racing. Berger conceded that he had backed off when he saw the red missile bearing down on him, lest there had been two cigarette-sponsored meteors visible on the Mexico City skyline that night.

Senna, meanwhile, remained a bit player in France while Prost took Ferrari's 100th win and his fifth at home ahead of the remarkable Ivan Capelli.

He repeated the feat at Silverstone, this time at the expense of Nigel Mansell. Having already got under the Englishman's skin with his political nous, it was also rumoured the Professor used Mansell's car, thinking it was a better chassis, without asking for permission first. When Prost did the unthinkable and deprived Mansell of a home win, it was too much for the implacable Brit, who announced he was retiring at the end of the season to spend more time with his family. It also emerged that Prost had betrayed team orders, which made his complaints after Imola the previous year look a little shallow.

Senna had made an unforced error and spun off, dropping him out of contention. As per 1989, he was encountering a mid-season lull and had been reduced to the deuteragonist in the title chase.

The problems partially lay in the car: the McLaren MP4–5B was a development of the previous year's dominant challenger but was finding itself outclassed in an area which then as now was and remains most crucial to a Grand Prix car – aerodynamics. On some circuits the 5B was peerless and yet on others it struggled.

The Ferraris of Prost and Mansell lacked the brute *banzai* grunt of the Honda but were making up for it with what was generally acknowledged as a better all round car. A consensus evidently shared by McLaren themselves, who blatantly copied it for 1991.

However, a concerted effort by McLaren as well as Japanese horsepower got the car back to the front for the German Grand Prix, but a decision to eschew a tyre stop saw Alessandro Nannini providing a challenge to Senna. He had to overtake the Italian to record his first win since Canada and retake the lead of the world championship.

Hungary was a weak track for McLaren for the second year running, and Williams locked out the front row. Nannini was again a barrier to Senna's success, but the Brazilian flipped the Benetton out of second position like a four-wheeled tiddlywink at the chicane, to the Italian's vocal disgust. He finished just inches behind Thierry Boutsen, who had led the whole race. Nigel Roebuck speculated that Senna had perhaps not employed the same tactics as he had used on the Italian because Boutsen and Senna were good friends, and it was obvious on the podium.

'It was a great day for me, it was not such a good day for him but I am sure he preferred to be beaten by me than by anybody else,' remembers Boutsen. 'He knew well that the car I was driving was not as good as his car and he congratulated me very sincerely.'

At the Belgian Grand Prix, Mansell coyly divulged if conditions were right, his wife and kids might have to wait another couple of years before he'd be joining them for family picnics spring and summer. Before long it was revealed that he had negotiated a deal to re-join Williams until the end of 1992, despite apparently demanding 'the impossible' from the team supremos.

Spa was always a venue for Senna demonstration runs and 1990 was no exception, despite the inconvenience of three starts after various scrapes, which Senna said made him wish he could just hit the kill switch and get into the nearest helicopter.

He didn't let that stop him taking a crucial win, just ahead of Prost, a result that was repeated at Monza. His lead in the championship was now 16 points.

The race was notable for the colossal accident that befell Lotus's Derek Warwick as he rounded Parabolica at the end of the first lap. The Englishman understeered exiting the right-hand sweep and ploughed into the tyre barrier at the track perimeter, ending up back in the middle of the road upside-down. Everyone behind streamed past and Warwick was able to clamber out and, after peering over the top of the wreckage to see there was nothing coming, run back to the pits and into the spare car. The man was nothing if not brave, but sadly that wasn't to be the end of the Lotus drivers' tribulations for the 1990 season.

Portugal provided Mansell with his first and only win of the season despite the buffoonery of Philippe Alliot who crashed right in front of him. Right behind Mansell, Senna took second and tightened his grip on that second world title. Surprisingly, it also turned out to be his last finish of the 1990 season.

Martin Donnelly's accident threw a giant shadow over the Spanish Grand Prix weekend. Despite Senna's heroics in qualifying, he was forced to retire from the race, which let Prost through to an essential win. Now Senna's advantage was not comfortable and the stage was for an incredible third successive showdown in Suzuka.

Senna was fastest in qualifying: no surprise there. But pole position hadn't served him well in Japan for the last two years and he felt the grid positioning ridiculous – how was it that the quickest man was not awarded the best opportunity to lead the race into the first corner? He decided to ask the stewards to allow him to start from the cleaner, faster side of the track. They agreed. But then Jean-Marie Balestre got wind of what was happening and refused to grant this request point blank.

It is worth clarifying that Balestre did not order a *change* to scupper Senna's chances, as has been suggested. Pole position had been sited on the drivers' right hand side for the previous three Grands Prix at Suzuka and Balestre merely saw no need to comply with a last-minute request from an uppity driver. If he complied, he arguably ran the risk of being seen to favour Senna. If he did not, he looked like he was bowing to Prost. In the end he decided to leave things as they had always been. Senna, unsurprisingly, didn't take to this news kindly, fuming:

'You break your balls to be on the pole and then they put you on the wrong side of the circuit to the benefit of whoever is in second place,' adding ominously: 'Maybe I am world champion before the race is finished ...'

At the green light, Prost did exactly what he had done 12 months before and surged into the lead. Senna, right behind him, kept his nose to the inside as Prost swung out wide to negotiate the first turn and ...'It's happened immediately!' screamed Murray Walker.

Wham! Both cars were in the sand trap, crumpled, out. The crash looked fairly similar to that at the start of the Brazilian GP the year before, but in that instance Senna had not intended to take Berger out of contention (although nor had he intended to let the Austrian past) and perhaps this led to Senna's defenders saying that he was only going for a gap left by Prost.

We now know, of course, Senna *did* cause the crash deliberately. It was arguably the lowest point of his career, in terms of sportsmanship. Here he took his unbending intransigence, his self-proclaimed will to win, but allied it to a level of angry single-mindedness that could easily have had disastrous consequences. It is even more astonishing when one considers that it came just weeks after Martin Donnelly's crash, which had shaken Senna to his core. And yet here he was inviting an even bigger disaster to befall one of his fellow drivers.

Two years later, at the same corner, Japanese Formula 3000 driver Hitoshi Ogawa suffered a horrific accident after making similar contact with rival Andrew Gilbert-Scott. He vaulted over the tyre wall and was killed instantly. What happened in 1990 could have easily been very similar: and it was instigated *with* intent.

Damon Hill watching on TV that weekend felt 'Senna had no regard for the other twenty-four guys behind on full fuel tanks. It was a completely selfish, irresponsible act.'

Derek Warwick said 'If Andrea de Cesaris [known for his consistent ability to find the scenery or other cars in his frequent off-track excursions] had pulled that he'd have been f*cked from here to kingdom come.'

Nigel Roebuck opined that 'it was a criminally irresponsible way of making a point – Prost's sheared-off rear wing could have come down anywhere – and for me remains the most reprehensible single action by a racing driver in the annals of the sport.'

Senna, as much he hated Prost on a professional level, must deep down have been thanking his lucky stars that the Ferrari driver was able to get out of his car and walk away. Prost was repulsed and even Senna himself was not happy with the manner in which he had won his second world championship.

'It is not only unsporting, it is disgusting,' spat the Frenchman 'He saw that I had made a better start and had a better car and he had no chance to win, so he pushed me off. I am not prepared to fight against irresponsible people who are not afraid to die.'

Ironically, after the FIA's punishment of Senna in 1989, he got off scot-free with what was quite obviously an infinitely more dangerous piece of driving, whether or not it was apparent at the time if it was deliberate or not.

'There were two factors,' he explained. 'One was to be out at the right time in terms of traffic and the other was, of course, Alain. I realised that the best situation to play at that stage was just to be slightly ahead of him. When I was ready to go, waiting, I was playing with him. When I heard their engine going on, I switched mine on and went, just to be ahead of him. It was a psychological factor – nothing else.'

Doodson says, 'I think Balestre learned something from '89 – in effect he realised that he had unfairly favoured Prost and he'd come off second best … it taught him not to get involved in any kind of dispute in which he might be accused of being partial. Senna probably got away with more in 1990 than he would have done if Balestre hadn't been so stupid in 1989.'

Balestre's successor, Max Mosley, told *Motorsport News* in 2002: 'Senna should probably have been excluded from the Championship for doing something that dangerous, but I think the feeling was that what happened the previous year was absolutely outrageous: that he genuinely won the race and it was taken away from him quite wrongly. So you couldn't help but have slight sympathy.'

In the furore, many forgot there was still a motor race going on. Gerhard Berger had been left with an untroubled lead but he spun off at the same spot where Senna and Prost clashed, leaving a delighted Nelson Piquet to score his first win for three years. His verdict on the championship defining incident? 'Senna just drove straight into the back of Prost, and that was it.'

Piquet was joined on the podium by overwhelmed compatriot Roberto Moreno, a replacement for Alessandro Nannini who had lost his right arm in a helicopter crash. The podium was completed by Larousse's Aguri Suzuki, the first Japanese driver to stand on the rostrum at his home race or indeed any other.

McLaren also clinched the Constructors' Championship in tandem with the drivers' title: the first 'hat trick' in the sport's history. But all eyes were on Senna and Prost.

'Well, what can you say about that?' Prost said many years later:

> After I'd retired we talked about it, and he admitted to me – as he did to the press – that he'd done it on purpose. He

explained to me why he did it. He was furious with Balestre for not agreeing to change the grid, so that he could start on the left, and he told me he had decided that if I got to the first corner ahead of him, he'd push me off.

What happened in Japan in '90 is something I will never forget, because it wasn't only Ayrton who was involved. Some of the people at McLaren, a lot of officials – and a lot of media – agreed with what he'd done, and that I couldn't accept. Honestly I almost retired after that race. As I always said, you know, he didn't want to beat me, metaphorically he wanted to destroy me – that was his motivation from the first day. Even in that Mercedes touring car race, back in '84, I realised that he wasn't interested in beating Alan Jones or Keke Rosberg or anyone else – it was me, just me, for some reason.

The matter was far from closed. At the season-closing Australian Grand Prix, Senna was asked by Jackie Stewart why, of all the world champions there had been, he was the one who seemed to be involved in the most crashes. Despite adopting a conciliatory smile, Senna was visibly bristling when questioned by Stewart, himself a proponent of Formula 1 safety and someone who wouldn't have caused a deliberate crash for all the Highland toffee in Scotland.

I find amazing for you to make such a question, Stewart. You are very experienced, you know a lot about racing. You should know that by being a racing driver, you are under risks all the time, it means you are racing with other people.

And if you no longer go for a gap that exists, you are no longer a racing driver, because we are competing to win.

I race to win. As long as I feel it's possible. It is impossible to get it right all the time. But I am designed to win. I can only do what speaks for my mind.

Stewart didn't buy it, and nor should he have done.

'This is all part of Senna's feeling that somehow standards for him were different from 'those applicable to other drivers', says Mike Doodson. 'None of us likes to have our faults pointed out to us, especially on TV.'

Prost refused to take part in both the end-of year drivers' photograph and a portrait of the surviving world champions, still furious over what had happened in Suzuka.

8

Titan of the Track

1991: Triple World Champion

The 1990 championship was not unlike the year before in that a tumultuous title race had ended with a bad taste in the mouth for all concerned. Being the aggressor rather than the victim didn't sit easily with Senna:

'It was a sh*t end to the world championship. It was not good for me and not good for F1.'

After his customary long break at home in Brazil for the southern summer, he returned to contest what he would later describe as 'the most competitive world championship that I have ever competed'. Although he would be as determined as ever to cream his rivals, one got the impression that Senna wanted 1991 to be as cleanly fought as possible.

1991 was the first year in which drivers in the world championship would keep every point they scored during the year, as opposed to the 'best eleven out of sixteen' rule that had attracted much criticism. Every result would count.

After the dominance of the first two seasons with Honda, McLaren had started to find itself outclassed in 1990 on certain tracks by the resurgence of the Steve Nichols–designed Ferrari, widely regarded as being aerodynamically superior. The new MP4/6 was indeed, as Senna wryly noted, a red and white tribute to the Ferrari 641, even featuring a V12 engine.

The new chassis was less peaky than its predecessor, but the new Honda powerplant was much heavier than the RA100EV10 and yet didn't produce quite enough power to offset the weight gain.

'Well before we went to the Phoenix GP, when we first tried the car in Portugal, I had two months off so I was fresh and full of motivation. I had a good feeling because we made a step forward in all areas but I didn't think we had done enough in some areas to be very confident,' Senna later said.

There was also the very serious threat of the resurgent Williams team. They had poached aerodynamicist Adrian Newey from Leyton House March, whose performances during 1988 and 1990 underlined what a talented designer the Englishman was. Renault's top brass were also determined to build upon the four wins they had garnered since their return to F1 and prove that they were the best in the business. Even the team's fuel supplier was rolling out the big guns: indeed the Elf fuel was so potent it actually caused deaths during development.

On top of this, Nigel Mansell was back where he always performed best: behind the wheel of 'Red Five'. Free from the shackles of Prost's politics at Maranello, he enjoyed clear number one status and a car designed with his bullish driving style in mind. Although incumbent Italian Riccardo Patrese was no batman, Nigel had first dibs on the best equipment.

Williams would however need time to get the promising FW14 to behave itself. One of its favourite tricks was to jump several gears mid-corner, throwing its surprised driver in the direction of the spectators' gallery. While the men from Didcot scrabbled, the man in the yellow crash helmet capitalised.

Senna's results from the first four races constituted the best start to an F1 campaign, and in a car that was not yet at its best. He won every single one while everyone else faltered: Mansell Patrese, Prost and Berger were all cursed with either unreliable or outdated cars.

Senna put the new McLaren on pole at Phoenix by over a second from Prost and 2.3 seconds ahead of teammate Berger. He then drove most of his last lap on Sunday waving to the crowd, miles ahead of anyone else. If the car really was as bad as he said it was, Senna's wasn't demonstrating it, but it wasn't quite as simple as it sounds.

The next race was in Brazil. On race day the atmosphere was electric, and the air rang in expectation of Senna's first win on home turf. The dedication among the fans there is found few places elsewhere – especially given the tickets cost at least a month's wages. Standing beside the world champion's car at the head of the grid, ESPN's John Bisignano felt every hair on his body stand on end.

As the race got under way the two Williams-Renaults looked threatening. Mansell provided the main menace in the early laps, but was never quite close enough to challenge before he was spinning like a gyroscope, out with gearbox trouble. Still if Senna thought he had an easy run to victory, fate, God, or his own gearbox were against him. His own gearbox was refusing to cooperate.

In the modern age of on-screen graphics displaying gear selection and engine revs, it would have been instantly apparent that something was seriously wrong with the McLaren and TV viewers would have expected him to throw in the towel within a couple of laps. As it was, no one apart from the McLaren team and Senna himself knew of the agonising struggle he was enduring to keep his car ahead of the chasing pack. But even with such a fundamental issue, this remained Senna's best chance of breaking his Brazilian jinx and he wasn't going to let it slip.

'The gearbox went completely crazy seven laps from the end. I couldn't believe it. I thought about it for one lap and decided to leave it in sixth, and drive around the circuit completely differently … in medium and slow speed sections it was a disaster. I changed my way of driving.'

The last few laps were absolute torture. Senna was now a much stronger driver than 'the wimp' of 1984 but nevertheless his slender frame was racked by agonising cramps from forcing the MP4/6 round corners in a gear that was only supposed to be used on the straights. His body cried 'enough'.

Then, the rain arrived. In the past, it had often provided Senna with the opportunity to overcome any shortcomings of his equipment, but not a broken gearbox. This was too much. He drove past the pits pointing furiously at the sky, urging the stewards to stop the race.

His calls were not heralded and he was forced to drive the entire race distance. But bad luck was also raining down on his rivals. Second-placed Patrese was experiencing gearbox troubles of his own, and teammate Berger, third, was having the wits scared out of him by a throttle that stayed wide open no matter what he was doing with the pedal. Senna was going to make it.

As he crossed the line his radio transmission to the team was one continuous yell: of pain, of exultation, of both. 'I don't f*cking believe it! We f*cking did it!'

Ron Dennis was visibly more exultant than usual, knowing how close Senna had come to losing the race. Senna's outburst took care of the last of his energy. He passed out in his car, although thankfully he stopped first. Even his father hugging him in the garage, after he was brought back in a track car, caused him to wince in pain.

On the podium his facial expression was a mixture of agony and unbridled pleasure. He could barely wave the Brazilian flag nor lift his victory trophy but, as with the win itself, he made sure he did so.

It was reminiscent of Nelson Piquet winning his first world title in 1981. At Caesar's Palace, in blistering heat, Piquet had spent most of the last lap vomiting and barely had the strength to lift his arm to celebrate his success as he crossed the line. But for Brazil and the Formula 1 world, this was a more iconic moment.

The next two races were straightforward and Senna won both, including at Monaco despite a marshal inexplicably deciding he had to cross the road right at Ste Devote precisely at the moment that Senna's McLaren was barrelling towards him.

'That marshal needs his brains testing!' shouted Murray Walker.

Doubtless the chap in question experienced an adrenaline rush that he has never experienced before or since, but it could have had spine-chilling echoes of the crash that killed Tom Pryce and marshal Jansen van Vuuren at Kyalami fourteen years previously if Senna had been two metres further up the road.

Senna now had 40 points and Mansell had 6. The odds for Williams success must have been rather attractive at Ladbrokes.

Even so, Senna wasn't kicking back in his private jet and cracking open the bubbly. 'We won the first four races and I kept saying to everyone "We're not there, we're not there" and many people were thinking "When is he going to be happy? Because he's on pole, he's winning, he's leading from first lap to last lap and he's complaining", but people inside the team knew, they understood.'

The first signs the 1991 title was not a foregone conclusion came in Canada, where the McLarens were outclassed by the Williams. Patrese took pole, outqualifying his supposed team leader for the fifth race in a row. One wag commented, 'Nigel will go back to his hotel room and kick his teddy bear.' Senna was only third on the grid, a lowly position for him, and retired with alternator failure.

Mansell, meanwhile, failed to capitalise on Senna's ill fortune by committing what was definitely the most embarrassing blunder of his career.

As he rounded his last lap, in the lead by a huge distance, he waved to the crowd in anticipation of an easy win – it isn't hard to suspect he was too busy doing this and not busy enough paying attention to his engine revs, and the Renault died on him as he was negotiating the hairpin. The reason given was, of course, gearbox failure, which if it was a fib was at least a plausible one given the past few races.

Mansell couldn't have chosen a man he'd like to inherit his win less – his old buddy Nelson Piquet, who was nevertheless gracious in victory, answering the query 'Do you feel sorry for Nigel?' with 'I don't feel sorry for nobody', adding 'I almost had an orgasm!'

Senna's preparations for the next race in Mexico were compromised before he arrived. In the interval between Grands Prix, he had been riding his jetski when he fell off and was given an impromptu haircut by the one behind. The back of his head required stitches and he needed to pay a visit to Sid Watkins to ensure that he was safe to drive. No sooner had he left the Prof behind than he was straight back to see him again: the curiously accident-prone world champion had tried to take Peraltada, the fearsome banked curve at the end of the lap, in sixth gear. With one hand off the wheel he found he could not hold the MP4/6 on line and he slid off the circuit and flipped at high speed. Thankfully, though careful to avoid stepping on pavement cracks for the rest of the weekend, he was unhurt and in an upbeat mood: 'I'm ready for another one tomorrow', he said.

Williams's strong form continued for the next few races while Senna racked up the points as best he could.

The German Grand Prix was the first for the country after reunification the previous October, but there would be no reconciliation in the F1 world with the Senna/Prost fallout that had last come to a head at Suzuka the same month making its presence known again.

With the Ferrari's pace being on the sluggish side in 1991, Senna had usually been too far ahead of Alain Prost to be bothered by him. But at Hockenheim the Ferrari was running as well as, if not better than, the McLaren. On lap 37, as Prost tried doggedly to pass his foe, some 'robust' defending from Senna sent the Frenchman up the escape road, where he promptly stalled after his clutch failed.

Prost was furious and made no bones about his intentions if he found himself in a similar position once again:

'I shall have no problems starting with him in Hungary, but if he gets in my way again I'll just have to push him off.'

Senna retorted, 'I think we all know by now that Prost is always complaining about something. It's never his fault.'

Prost wasn't Senna's only worry. To cap an irritating weekend, his car also ran out of fuel for the second race in succession. He stalked back to the pits and confronted Ron Dennis, perhaps an early indication that he would not remain at McLaren for the rest of his days. The frustration at finding himself with inferior machinery and bearing the brunt of silly mistakes was starting to make itself apparent.

'One thing I have learned lately is that you should monitor very carefully your words, particularly if it's not your native language,' he later admitted, 'but I am afraid that on that occasion, in the back of the McLaren truck, I was not monitoring my words at all!'

Before the race in Hungary the FIA shoved Prost and Senna in front of the press and made the pair trot out rehearsed statements of contrition that made pro-wrestling look spontaneous. Prost had a crack at looking like he was at least trying to seem remorseful, but Senna shook his hand with the air of a man with a knife pressed into his back.

Nevertheless, it worked. In the wake of Prost's comments at Hockenheim, *Autosport* had suggested that for once the Professor had not been thinking straight as the blame for any future clashes would automatically be pinned on him. And yet the events in Germany constituted the last true Senna/Prost confrontation.

As the circus arrived at Spa, there had been upheaval at the Jordan team, whose misfortunes would have a massive bearing on the next 21 years, and counting, of Grand Prix racing. Their regular driver Bertrand Gachot had apparently taken a London cabbie's bartering the wrong way and blasted CS gas in his face, leaving him in a prison cell rather than the cockpit of his 191.

Eddie Jordan looked to the Sauber-Mercedes sportscar team and one of its drivers, a 22-year-old German by the name of Michael Schumacher, to fill one of his 7UP branded cars. Schumacher escaped nobody's attention by qualifying eighth, which became seventh when the Williams of Patrese was hoofed off the front row for not having a working reverse gear. Schumacher's race ended at the first corner when he burnt his clutch out leaving Le Source, but he would figure in Senna's life in a major way over the next three seasons.

Senna won again on the Sunday, but it wasn't his usual dominant performance and he inherited the victory only when Mansell and Alesi ahead suffered mechanical troubles.

And yet, with two victories in succession, his lead in the championship had gone from being slightly anaemic to full strength once more. It now stretched to 22 points since Mansell had retired from a seemingly unthreatened position at the front with electrical gremlins.

The pendulum swung in Williams's favour again at Monza, although at a track which definitely favoured the Canon-branded cars the Brazilian was fearsome. He took an unlikely pole but first Patrese and then Mansell passed him. Patrese then spun into the sand, while Mansell held on for his fourth win of the year to just keep his fans on tenterhooks for a little longer. Senna drove with a controlled fury and fought up back to second, having dropped back when changing tyres.

Yet, Portugal was a disastrous race for Mansell. He was forced to aggressively chop across the bows of both McLarens at the start after a tardy getaway and at his first pit stop, his Williams mechanics failed to attach his right rear wheel properly and the FW14 turned into a tricycle in the middle of the pit lane. Mansell remembered his mistake from the same race two years previously and didn't engage reverse. He just sat in his car swearing instead.

His crew ran over to the car and lifted it off the ground by the rear wing, which was highly illegal. Eventually he roared off but, inevitably, Red Five got the Black Flag, leaving the victory on a platter for a grateful Patrese. The man in second place may have been, as he famously proclaimed, the first of the losers, but Senna didn't seem too downbeat about it. 'Six points', was the succinct answer when he was asked what his finish meant to him. He could smell his third championship.

In spite of being so close to the world championship, Senna was strangely off-colour at the new Catalunya circuit. He was beaten to pole by Gerhard Berger and incredibly admitted that 'he lacked a little bit of commitment'.

Before the race started there were harsh words between Senna and Mansell in the drivers' briefing. Mansell had not taken kindly to being told, in indirect terms, that he would face a ban if he tried another start-line *banzai* like he had in Portugal, and in the manner of the playground had pointed at Senna and said 'He does it too!'

Senna, level-headed as always, told Mansell in no uncertain terms what he thought of him. Although the exact quote has gone unrecorded, it is believed that it wasn't very nice. 'A kindergarten full of millionaires', was the verdict of one unimpressed witness.

At the same briefing, Nelson Piquet had some strangely prescient words to say on the matter which had so enraged his two favourite colleagues: safety. He said, with some feeling, that someone would have to be killed before the FIA would introduce any significant safety measures. He was sadly to be proved right before long.

So there was bad blood for race day and Senna was famously bested in a wheel-to-wheel contest with Mansell as they both tried to outdrag each other down the main straight, later telling

Mansell (to the Brit's delight) that he was 'f*cking crazy'. He spun at the last corner for good measure and sulked 'I don't know why Mansell is doing what he is doing', finishing a muted fifth.

Suzuka, Joe Saward wrote at the time, had an atmosphere of foreboding in the days building up to the race, although the weekend got off to a light-hearted start when Senna discovered hundreds of eager Japanese noses pressed up against the window of his motorhome as he was getting changed. His blind-closing was allegedly as swift as his driving.

For the fourth year in a row, the championship could be decided here and given the controversy of 1989 and 1990, Senna could have been forgiven for wondering if there were more fireworks en route. Certainly that was what everyone else seemed to be thinking.

Mansell still needed to win the next two races with Senna not scoring to lift his first world title, and with Senna only having suffered one mechanical failure during the previous seventeen races, Mansell must have been in the market for a few rabbits' feet.

Sadly, in the end the anticipated crackle of fireworks was more reminiscent of spent bubble wrap. On lap ten as he was harrying Senna, Mansell went too deep into the first corner and ploughed into the sand, not to re-emerge, and Senna became the youngest ever triple world champion.

Job done, he immediately hammered out a lap that was almost two seconds faster than he had gone before, with the impressive Berger in front of him.

Berger was well on course to win the race on his own merits, but he waved the new world champion through. They then ran in formation until the final lap, when Senna decided to let Berger through again at the final chicane as a present for all his support over the past two seasons. Berger looked happy enough on the top step of the podium, although it was all a tad contrived for some people who muttered that Senna had made the gesture with bad grace.

However, this was nothing compared to the post-race press conference. Clearly still gnawed by the memories of the previous two seasons, the Brazilian launched an embittered attack against outgoing FIA president Jean-Marie Balestre, who had been succeeded by Max Mosley before the Spanish GP.

> It's been a memorable championship, not only for me, but I think Formula 1 over the past few years. Past two years were 89, with a disgraceful end when I won the race and I've missed one victory in my career. That '89 I won, and it was taken away. I was prevented to go to the podium when I was just about to go to it, by Balestre. And I'll never forget that.

> A result of that was the 1990 championship, when we fought all the way, myself and Prost, 'til we came to the last race. Pole position was set in the wrong place. We agreed before we started qualifying that pole would be on the outside, with the officials. Then Balestre gave the order after qualifying to not change, and I found myself on the wrong side on pole. I was so frustrated that I promised myself that if, after the start, I lose first place I would go for it in the first corner, regardless of the result, I would go for it and Prost wouldn't turn into the first corner ahead of me. That's what took place. That was a result of the politicians making stupid decisions, bad decisions.

Senna didn't miss the opportunity to have a gentle pop at Mansell either: 'This year, what happened was that we fought all the way, myself, Nigel and Riccardo, and we got to the end and it was only myself and Mansell. We had a hard time in the last two races, I think Mansell pushed a little over the limit, but I was able to compensate for it and avoid incidents and a bad fight for the championship.'

Despite his outburst attracting criticism, Senna got what he wanted: a clean and largely controversy-free third title. He had also shown he was not, as Alain Prost alleged, a driver who only knew how to go hell-for-leather the whole time. This was a calmer and more mature Senna, who had collected valuable points on the days when his McLaren was outclassed and made the most of matters when it was not.

As it had been every year since the race's inception in 1987, the title had been settled at Suzuka. Constructors' trophy ambitions aside, there was an end of term atmosphere in Australia.

Senna, reportedly, enjoyed success off the track as well as on that weekend. The supermodel Elle 'The Body' Macpherson was invited by BMW to give the pre-Grand Prix celebrity race a little more glamour, and Senna took it upon himself to ensure that she was as comfortable as possible while she was harmlessly tooling around at the back of the field. His very thorough debriefing before and after the race were captured, unbeknown to him, by the TV cameras. In typical fashion it was none other than Gerhard Berger who made a few 'nudge, nudge' suggestions and Senna went as red as his overalls. If one believes the rumours Berger's ribbing had some resonance.

The rain, an unanticipated aberration, wasn't the only disruption in Adelaide. Alain Prost, not known for withholding comments if he felt disgruntled about something, had publicly likened his Ferrari to a haulage vehicle and was promptly relieved of his seat, meaning that he was without a drive for 1992. He was replaced by the team's test driver Gianni Morbidelli.

Adelaide 1991 remains the shortest Grand Prix to have been contested to date. After 17 laps there were more racing car components littering the track than competing vehicles. Senna, who started from pole, had already managed to lap some drivers twice but even he thought this was ridiculous and drove around waving an infuriated arm at the stewards. For once his protests were heeded and out came the red flag. Nigel Mansell, in second place, added injury to the ignominy of being beaten to the title and aquaplaned into the wall, breaking his foot. Initially there was concern for his welfare as he remained in the Williams, immobile, but when Sid Watkins leaned into the cockpit and asked him why, Mansell said, 'Cos it's raining!'

He was still awarded second but was unable to take his place on the podium along with the two McLarens. They had helped their team to the Constructors' Championship in the face of an extremely strong challenge from Williams, but there was no escaping the fact the event was a poor platform for Senna to celebrate becoming the youngest-ever triple world champion. Nevertheless, Senna's summary showed how much he valued his personal achievement and that of his team: 'It's been the most competitive world championship that I have ever competed, because we fought with different cars, different engines, different drivers, not inside the same team, therefore it was really tough. We started the year well but then we had a tough time from the fourth race onwards as you all know.'

1992–1993: The Underdog

Pre-season Senna had told the audience at the *Autosport* awards:

'I think it could be an even more exciting championship compared to 1991... I think '92 could be a continuity of '91, hopefully not with the same struggle as we had halfway this year and hopefully I can go back to the pits every time after the race with my racing car and not with a lift or the pace car!'

Sadly the 1992 championship was anything but exciting. With no Prost and no Piquet, the line-up was missing some star power even with the presence of Senna and Mansell, leading Jean Alesi to say that he felt like 'an orphan'. From the first practice session it was obvious the Williams FW14B was vastly superior to anything else regardless of the conditions and even Senna's talent wouldn't be enough to allow him to compete on an even keel.

There were only three wins for him all year: at Monaco he inherited the lead when the dominant Mansell was forced to call into the pits with a suspected puncture, but his defence was masterful when the Williams was swarming all over the back of his McLaren as the lap counter wound down. Mansell now says, without rancour, that in this day and age Senna's blocking manoeuvres would have earned him two stop and go penalties: a criticism of today's over-regulated F1 than of his rival's driving.

In Hungary Senna finished ahead of Mansell again, the Englishman taking second place and with it the title he had wanted so badly after twelve years of trying. On the podium Senna leant over to his successor to congratulate him, giving a fascinating insight into his *modus operandi*:

'It's such a good feeling, isn't it? Now you know why I'm such a b*****d. I don't ever want to lose the feeling or let anybody else experience it.'

There were a couple of moments of controversy involving the pair throughout the year. In Canada Mansell clashed with the Brazilian and in Adelaide the pair took each other off, Mansell claiming that he had been brake-tested by his rival and Senna that Nigel had simply braked too early. It was the last time we would see the two of them together on a racetrack.

Monza saw the final win for the Senna/McLaren-Honda combination. When thanked by the Japanese company for all he had achieved with them, Senna was moved to tears. But he remained a hard-nosed professional. While he was evidently disgusted by Prost's actions in vetoing him from the Williams team for 1993, he made it no secret he was contemplating a year's sabbatical if he could not get himself into a competitive seat for the next year:

> I wouldn't be prepared to continue driving next year unless I felt I could compete, and that meant not that I had to leave McLaren or anything, but if you feel you

have light at the end of the tunnel in which you can work and be back in a competitive way, and if that situation did not turn up for me then I wouldn't drive, without really wishing to stop. I am only 32 and there's no sense for me to stop. The peak of my career has a good few years ahead. I have achieved so much credibility and experience that it's not the time to stop.

On the other hand, there is no sense to just be a number out there, given the fact that whether you're fighting for first or second, fifth or sixth, you're exposing yourself to a lot of danger continuously, a lot of stress, and a lifestyle that is not always attractive for me.

Anything else I could not justify to myself. I know the feeling when you don't want to retire and you have to go that direction.

Senna briefly considered a move to the IndyCar series and tested a Penske at Phoenix in a test arranged by Emerson Fittipaldi, who was himself still racing in the series with great success many years after retiring from Formula 1. Senna told the media:

'I think racing cars are like drugs in my blood and when I got really close I felt that very special feeling. They started to warm up the engine and I think the bug has woken up inside me after being a little numb.'

But those closest to him reckoned he wasn't really serious and after the test he went on his way again, never to return.

Nonetheless, Ron Dennis had felt nervous enough in the interim to try and force Senna's hand, and signed promising former Lotus racer Mika Hakkinen to partner 1991 IndyCar champ Michael Andretti, son of Mario, to cover his back while his star driver dilly-dallied.

Senna still deigned to test the new MP4/8, even though he was unsure what he would do, but eventually agreed to drive on a race for race basis.

With Honda gone, McLaren were stuck with a customer supply of Ford engines, and not even the best ones available. The Benetton team were the works Ford outfit and were contractually entitled to the latest spec units. It was incredible that a team of McLaren's calibre found itself in such a situation. It was reminiscent of Williams's 1988 season, when even as the champion constructor they had to buy customer Judd engines.

Senna was a man who ten years before had thought nothing of driving to Novamotor in Italy with his F3 engine on the back seat to make sure he had the best possible powerplant, and did not take being forced to accept a disadvantage lightly.

For the '93 season Williams looked well placed once again. While Mansell decided not to stay after his wage demands were rejected by his notoriously parsimonious boss, and Riccardo Patrese had agreed to join Benetton, refusing to renege on a deal already agreed upon, the new driver lineup of the returning Alain Prost and former test driver Damon Hill, a refugee from the embers of the old Brabham team, was very competitive.

The team were a year ahead of their chief opponents in other crucial areas – the active suspension and traction control systems that made the FW14B so dominant were now housed in the much sleeker and purpose-built '15C.

The 14B, had been an evolution of a passively-suspended car. The 15C was honed to perfection.

Still, round one in Kyalami gave F1 fans a welcome reminder of the intense Prost/Senna rivalry that had been lacking for the previous two years, for different reasons.

Senna seemed reinvigorated by the return of his old nemesis, parrying with Prost for several laps before the Williams's superiority made itself felt. As the race drew to a conclusion the heavens opened and Prost made it clear that he wanted the race stopped, but he held on to take his first victory since the 1990 Spanish Grand Prix. Senna finished second. It was like they'd never been apart.

As the field headed to Brazil few would have put money on Senna taking his second home victory as he ended qualifying a laughable 2.824s behind Prost on the grid.

Ironically achieving his goal was much less painful this time around for Senna, in spite of his car's apparent deficiencies. Whereas he had famously battled gearbox problems two years earlier and ended up passing out in agony, this time victory was comparatively easy. The rain that so often levelled out the field fell with a vengeance on lap 29 and Prost was powerless to stop his car sliding off the circuit in tandem with the Minardi of Christian Fittipaldi ahead of him.

Stymied by the safety car, Hill's huge lead was lost and Senna pounced, going on to win by sixteen seconds. This time, with a functioning gearbox, the delighted Brazilian had energy in reserve to enjoy his victory and hung out the window of a course car, waving a *bandeira,* as he was driven round Interlagos.

To make his second home victory that little bit more special, Senna's trophy was presented by his idol, the legendary Juan Manuel Fangio, a man for whom Senna would have dropped everything. Once in the Interlagos paddock, Nigel Roebuck had seen Fangio come up and tap Senna on the shoulder mid-conversation. Senna swung around ready to give the source of the interruption a piece of his mind, but when he saw it was Fangio tears sprang to his eyes. As he stood on the podium now, he jumped off the step and one legend embraced another. This was a far cry from the usual sterile handshakes with obscure foreign dignitaries.

The third round of the season would end up as the stage for what most regard as Senna's finest performance (mystifyingly reduced to a post-ending footnote in Asif Kapadia's *Senna* film).

The 1993 European Grand Prix was voted by the readers of *Autosport* as the greatest race of the 20th century, which gives an idea of the esteem in which it is held. But it was not a race at all. It was a demonstration run for Senna. It was an exercise in sticking two fingers up at his opposition. Had the poll been to find the greatest *performance* of the 20th century, then this exalted position would be almost unquestionable.

Donington Park's owner Tom Wheatcroft had seen the Auto Union victories of Rosemeyer and Nuvolari in 1937 and '38 and was determined to bring Formula 1 back to the track that he had bought in 1971.

After an unsuccessful pitch for the British Grand Prix was rebuffed, the failure of a proposed race at the Japanese Autopolis circuit meant that the stage was set for the mutton-chopped Wheatcroft to realise his dream.

There were no surprises in dry qualifying as the Williams locked out the front row, with Schumacher's more powerful Benetton third and Senna's McLaren only fourth.

Come race day though, things were different. The crowd at the circuit was small, as the paying public neither trusted the weather nor guessed what was to follow.

The sponsors of the event, the Japanese computer games manufacturer Sega, may well have believed that the Williams team to which they also gave their backing would provide them with a clean sweep.

On race day, Easter Sunday, the conditions were wet, so already the threat from Schumacher's Benetton looked weaker as his B193 was not fitted with the traction control that it needed to stay in the hunt. The German sighed and ran his hand through his mullet, he looked troubled; contrastingly, Senna, sitting in the car with his helmet on, playfully waggling his hands either side of his head in a cheeky gesture to some unseen beneficiary, did not. A playful sticker on the cowling of his McLaren cockpit showed a cartoon hedgehog, strangely reminiscent of Sega's Sonic mascot, with a tyre-track through it: no prizes for guessing what that was meant to symbolise.

Murray Walker told BBC viewers he had a feeling Senna would liven up proceedings in the conditions. And he wasn't wrong.

At the green light both Williams got away cleanly, but Senna was momentarily passed by Karl Wendlinger's Sauber, which made a great start to go from fifth to third. Then he set about reeling off what was arguably the most iconic lap of his career, and perhaps even of Formula 1.

He was alongside Schumacher almost immediately and dispatched him as he turned into Redgate before driving around Wendlinger on the *outside* of the Craner Curves, displaying tenacity and feel apparently lacking in the drivers of the other twenty-four cars.

He gave second-placed Hill a choice of being overtaken or going into the gravel at McLean's and then scythed up the inside of Prost at the Melbourne hairpin. He had gone from fifth to first in less than a lap.

The McLaren was moving as though it were a Scalextric car slotted into the road while elsewhere everyone slithered around.

As the track periodically dried, Prost was able to use his Williams's superiority to close the gap, but the rain would then again arrive with vigour. Although, he didn't mention such matters this time (probably having been stung by criticism in the past) Senna really seemed to have God on his side on a day of such religious significance.

There was the minor setback of a botched pit stop, which saw the agitated visor-flipping Senna demonstrated on such occasions; he was also nearly wiped off the road by Christian Fittipaldi as he lapped him, but no matter what they threw at him his dominance was never challenged. As he crossed the line his fist punched the air and was held there in a gesture of what seemed like defiance rather than outright delight. He only fluffed one aspect of the entire weekend – on his victory lap he dropped the *bandeira* that he had been given to wave.

That he owed his win to his undeniable talent is not in doubt, but the margin of his victory also owed something to the incompetence of his closest rivals. Schumacher spun out on lap 22. Prost and Hill got their set-ups wrong and the Frenchman seemed to spend more time in the pits than he did on track, eventually making a record seven stops as he was constantly caught out by the rain. He also stalled his engine for good measure while trying to pull away from one pitstop, costing him valuable time. The look of frustration was evident through his crash helmet's aperture as he eventually roared off into the distance. Prost was lapped by Senna, which was something he wasn't used to, and beaten by Hill into the bargain.

In the post-race press conference, Mike Doodson recalls, Senna brought the house down.

'Prost was going through all the things that had gone wrong. The tyres were cold because they weren't in the blankets for long enough, etc.

'Senna was sitting behind him getting more and more annoyed, until he said "Why don't we swap cars?"'

Nigel Roebuck was of the opinion that the quip had a nasty side to it, but many others agreed the Brazilian had a point.

Not even the questionable trophy, a Sega-sponsored figurine of Sonic the Hedgehog, could dampen Senna's spirits.

Interviewed the same year, he said 'It was great, it was great. We lapped everybody; we could have won the race with one lap over everybody. It didn't happen in the end because we just slowed down. I don't remember a Grand Prix that was won in such a style. There you go, it was one of those days that everything came together between the driver and the team, the circumstances on the circuit, the pit stops the information, the strategy, and there we put together an incredible and fascinating result.'

By now Senna was leading the championship against all the odds and the world turned its attention to Prost, who looked like a novice in comparison. With the same equipment advantage as Mansell had enjoyed twelve months before, he had amassed less than half the Englishman's points up to the same juncture in the season.

Monaco witnessed the last of Senna's record six triumphs in the principality. He was uncharacteristically scruffy in practice and spun off several times in his pursuit of the limit, and on race day he was gifted a win. Rather like the year before, it took the misfortune of his rivals to put him in the lead.

Michael Schumacher, who would himself win in Monte Carlo five times in the future, was comfortably out in front when his hydraulic system grenaded.

To this day Senna's Monaco win tally remains the only record of any worth that remains unbeaten, despite the success of the Schumacher juggernaut in the following decade. Perhaps this, more than anything, underlines what a talent he was even though his other records have all been surpassed.

After the Canadian race Senna and the rest of the F1 fraternity were shocked by the sudden death of BBC commentator and 1976 champion James Hunt at the age of only 45. Senna offered his own tribute-of-sorts to the man who had commentated on the whole of his F1 career, although he could have been talking about someone else …

'He was not very interested about other people's opinion. He believed very much in his own values and his own reasons and whether they were sometimes making people uncomfortable or not was not a problem for him. In fact sometimes he was even capable of even going too far … it was his nature and his character.'

The next few races betrayed the McLaren's inferiority and Senna was left to make up the lower-ranked points scorers. It was not until much later in the year that he would remind the world what he was capable of.

The question of relative superiority of certain cars has been a constant topic of debate in Formula 1. On the one hand, manufacturers should be allowed to build their own cars and inevitably one group of engineers may interpret the rules more successfully than another. On the opposite side of the coin, it makes the sport dull for the casual viewer if one team steals a march on their competitors and the driver's role becomes less relevant.

James Hunt once discussed this phenomenon. 'It makes a mockery of Grand Prix racing … it's utterly demoralising for any world class driver who has that indignity inflicted upon him. Grand Prix racing should be trying to make the cars equal, not allow for further ingenious ways around the rules in order to make for good racing. It's a sad thing to see two cars in front with all the rest of them running along, all huffing and puffing in quite breathless pursuit.'

When Nigel Mansell was talking about his comeback for 1991 after his aborted retirement, he was careful to mention that while he would not wish his ideal car to be uncompetitive in any way, nor would he like it to be noticeably superior to any of the others on the grid.

Sadly, even a driver with the undoubted natural talent of Ayrton Senna had realised the year before that life in Formula 1 is no fun when a driver with infinitely less experience can simply drive past you:

> The machines have taken away the character and it is the character that the sponsors and public are looking for. At the top, you have a few characters of conflicting person-ality; the rest, without good results, don't have any credibility. We must reduce costs so that we return to an era where the emphasis is on people not computers.
>
> I want to be challenged by my own limits and by someone who is made of the same skin and bone and

where the difference is between brain and experience and adaptation to 'the course. I do not want to be challenged by someone else's computer. If I give 100% to my driving, which is my hobby as well as my profession, I can compete with anyone, but not computers.

Up until 1992 – 1993 Senna's berths in each of his teams were borne of good judgement. 1984 was spent with Toleman, a team with whom he felt he could learn valuable lessons out of the glare of a hotshot teammate and expectant team bosses. Lotus provided him with a quick car and malleable team environment, McLaren had given him a series of world-class winning machines.

But now, for the first time, he seemed unable to control his destiny. He was getting left behind and there was precious little he could do about it. He told Joe Saward that he was now enjoying racing 'a lot less' than he used to.

In his desperation Senna was even more determined to join the Williams team for 1994, and badgered Frank Williams with constant phone calls that must have enabled his telecoms provider to retire ten years early. Renault also had Frank's ear and began to make overtures about a return to the glory years of Senna and Prost in the same team once more.

Alain Prost got wind of this and took decisive action. He announced his retirement from Formula 1 at the start of the Portuguese weekend, one year after the infamous press confer-ence in which Senna had poured scorn upon him. He simply could not face the thought of the pressure-cooker atmosphere that would have resulted from his nemesis elbowing his way, once again, into the affections of Prost's team.

He later said, 'I did not want to be teammates with Ayrton again. I did not want to continue with this perception of people saying 'Ayrton is a poor guy with the small car, and when Alain wins it is normal because he has the best car … I said OK, you pay me the contract for next year and I stop … I really did not want to stop.'

This cleared the way for Senna to take over the number 2 Williams seat for 1994, a move that nobody doubted would deliver him his fourth world title and his first for three years.

Senna's race at Monza was scruffy and was a rare occasion where he retired due to an unforced error. Having hit Hill at the start and dropped back, he then drop-kicked his old F3 nemesis Martin Brundle out of the race at the second chicane. Ten years after their duel at Oulton Park, they were still getting in each other's way.

Senna triumphed at Suzuka, despite his altercation with Eddie Irvine, having qualified an impressive second.

The final race of the season was the Australian Grand Prix at Adelaide, a circuit at which Senna had surprisingly only won once before. Yet it served as a perfect bookend to his McLaren career.

He denied Williams a clean sweep of pole positions with a 1:13:371, four-tenths ahead of Prost. What was even more incredible was that he spent his whole lap trying to fiddle with his broken radio. This meant he failed to hear the voices of Ron Dennis and race engineer Giorgio Ascanelli telling him to slow down! In the pits afterwards his bemused boss patted him on the back and said, 'Just as well the radio button stuck. Jesus Christ!'

He was set to make his swansong for McLaren a memorable one. In the post-qualifying press conference he glanced at third-fastest Damon Hill and quipped 'I'm going to have a word with Frank about some team orders for tomorrow.' It raised a chuckle, although funnily enough not from Hill, who didn't look impressed.

As it transpired, Senna needed nobody's assistance.

Before the race he and Ron Dennis agreed to put their differences aside and do what was best for both of them: and that's exactly what Senna did. The relationship that had delivered so much success had soured, with rumours of Dennis saying Senna was unemployable getting the Brazilian's heckles raised.

Perhaps it was unsurprising that this happened, given Senna's increasingly unreasonable demands. Gerhard Berger, as well he as he got on with Senna on a personal level, was always amazed at how much leeway he had within McLaren.

'That was the strange thing: Ron has quite a strong character, you know, but Ayrton always told him what to do. I remember occasions when he said things to him that I just couldn't believe, but Ron accepted anything from Ayrton. If you ask him, I'm sure he will say no, it's not true, and maybe he believes it. But, from the outside, there was no doubt about it.'

Remembers Dennis:

The night before and the night after that race we talked about whether we should try and extract him from his contractual obligations to stay at McLaren. The car was particularly good and he had regained confidence in McLaren's ability to provide him with a winning car.

But by the time that post-race evening had finished, I think neither of us was particularly lucid! It had lapsed into emotion. He was an honourable guy and he had made a commitment to Williams. While he definitely reviewed it, I don't think there was any set of circumstances that would lead him to renege on his word.

The fact that he had done such an exceptional job in the closing stages of the season it was very difficult to get upset.

There had been moves afoot to secure a Lamborghini V12 supply for McLaren in time for 1994, but it came to nothing, in spite of Senna's praise for the engine during two tests. It mattered little anyway, as he was going where he wanted: Williams.

9

1994

It had been Frank Williams who had given Senna his first ever try-out in an F1 car ten and a half years earlier and now Senna had come full circle. Williams himself, at least, saw it as inevitable.

Senna's signing had not come as a colossal surprise: even on the day Nigel Mansell won the 1992 world title Senna had irked Williams by trying to talk to him about his own prospects for the next year when there was, instead, some partying to be done.

The driving aids of which Senna had been such a vocal opponent had been outlawed for the new season, meaning that the cars were now something approaching what they had been like in 1991.

In January Senna travelled to Estoril with his new teammate Damon Hill. The lead driver wasn't the only change to be presented to the media that day: the familiar blue, yellow and white Canon branding had given way to the colours of the Rothmans cigarette brand.

The cars on display were the 1993 cars modified to feature passive suspension, as per the new rules, but the new FW16 was soon ready.

Upon its launch Adrian Newey was confident the car would deliver both titles yet again, and pointed to innovations like an unusual anhedral rear wing element and tighter packaging of bodywork to back up his assertions. But the '16 was nowhere near as good as either of its dominant predecessors, despite outward appearances. Aerodynamically the car was flawed, with silly faults such as a poorly-calibrated front wing that would not be addressed until Imola.

All the other ingredients for a successful team were in place – Senna, Newey and the brute power of the Renault V10 – but the new car was a skittish beast that was difficult to set up and most tellingly, to drive on the limit.

Before long it was apparent that Williams's advantage from the past two years seemed to have gone, and Senna must have been drumming his fingers on the table. He had joined the team in order to marry his peerless talent with peerless machinery, not to flail round playing the unhappy underdog for a third season. He had been right to leave McLaren, as their appalling partnership with Peugeot that year proved, and yet the goalposts had moved yet again. Suddenly the Benetton team, who had been decent but unspectacular performers in 1993, looked to have built the quickest car.

Biographer Richard Williams says, 'His instinct let him down. Probably given the parameters, it was the right decision, and you would go back and look at the conditions and come to exactly that decision. It happened to be the wrong one. But there was no way he could have known that until he actually stepped into the Williams for the first time in 1994.'

'Even great drivers make mistakes with their movements,' says Mike Doodson. 'The only driver who chose unerringly where to go was Fangio.'

The season started in Interlagos and there was reason for cautious optimism when the home favourite got pole position there for the first time since 1991. Perhaps the car wasn't as bad as it was made out.

Good over one lap in the hands of the qualifying master it may have been, but in the race the FW16 was a different proposition entirely. Despite leading early on, Senna was overtaken in the pit stops by Schumacher, who had fallen to third early on. He refused to give up and slowly but surely reeled in the Benetton, but an uncharacteristic spin on lap 56 at Junção showed how hard he had been pushing. Despite a shove from the marshals his race was over. He was driving the car as fast as it would go, so much so that he was a lap ahead of a disbelieving Hill in the sister car.

Senna was not sure that Benetton's leap forward was entirely down to an intrinsically good design, and while he unusually kept his opinions to himself in public, he was quick to share them in private. Among Senna's confidantes was Prost: 'He was convinced that Benetton was cheating. He was very upset about that.' Specifically Senna thought the Enstone team was using traction and launch control software, which was now illegal. If this was true, they perhaps were not the only ones, as Ferrari substitute driver Nicola Larini also let slip about using such a system in the build up to the second race of the season at the Japanese circuit of Aida.

Again, Senna got pole, although he and Hill demonstrated the twitchiness of their mounts with identical spins on the tight little track, more suitable for karts than red-blooded Grand Prix cars. But that's as far as the celebrations went.

As Flavio Briatore approached him to wish him luck for the race, Senna forced an unenthusiastic smile. But he did look, as his old friend and Formula Ford team boss Dennis Rushen noticed, like he just couldn't be bothered any more. Many would say he seemed the same two weeks later. Keith Sutton says 'The problem was that the car wasn't quick enough, or, as has been proven, the Benetton had some trick software. I think he was frustrated that he couldn't keep up with Schumacher.'

Prost agrees: 'He was obviously not very happy with the performance of the car. He was saying that he could not find the motivation against Michael and the other drivers. He was really like ... if he had not lost his passion, he had problems with the car, the team, safety, some personal problems ... he had lost his skill and that was very surprising.'

Ron Dennis thinks Senna's unhappiness was more deep-rooted than mere car issues. 'It was very apparent to me, Josef Leberer and one of his closest friends, Sid Watkins … all three of us formed the opinion that Ayrton quickly regretted leaving the team. Not specifically because of competitiveness or uncompetitiveness, but more because he didn't expect to find himself in such a different culture and one that was quite alien to the way he was.'

When the green flag fell on Sunday, Senna made a poor start, fishtailing as he struggled to put the power down, and was immediately passed by Schumacher. He was then rammed off the track by his former teammate Hakkinen and T-boned for good measure by Larini, who was standing in for the injured Jean Alesi in the Ferrari. The front right suspension, something that would tragically feature two weeks later, was ruined and he was out before the end of the first lap.

He stormed back to the Williams pit, with the apologetic Larini in tow, stopping to complain to the stewards while he was at it to bemoan the apparent deterioration in driving standards. He was also keen to observe the suspect behaviour of Schumacher's car through the twisty bits. The German won again: 20–0 to Michael.

Imola

Senna arrived in Bologna on Thursday 28th April to begin his preparations for the San Marino Grand Prix, a race he liked and had won three times previously. He was there on business, mindful of his life after Grand Prix racing, helping to launch a Senna-branded mountain bike. The 'double-S' Senna logo has appeared on the front wing supports of every Williams F1 car since 1995.

He was also distracted by his family's attitude to his personal life, particularly his girlfriend Adriane. His younger brother

Leonardo had been dispatched by Mission Control in Sao Paulo to tell him that a 21-year-old Hungarian-Brazilian model wasn't the right sort of girl for him and he should promptly ditch her.

Senna had appeared in glossy lifestyle magazines with Adriane, both of them wearing nothing but tiny swimming costumes and a smile. Milton da Silva nearly had a fit when he saw the pictures, and made his displeasure known to his elder son. But Senna was a man who had been used to listening to the man he still called 'Daddy' for long enough, and was perhaps thinking at 34, he should probably be making a few more decisions himself.

He was a long way from the young man with the gawky smile that Keith Sutton had first encountered thirteen years earlier: '[I saw him] on Thursday, when he arrived in the paddock, when he was chatting to Rubens [Barrichello], I got some nice shots of the two of them. Just a quick chat, no conversation. By that time we were just two professional people doing our jobs.'

Senna's prospects for the race looked better than they had in either of the first two rounds. In its 1994 configuration Imola's long sweeping corners suited the power of the Renault engine, and Williams had made some tweaks to the FW16. These included modifications to the cockpit cowling to make Senna and Hill more comfortable, and the Brazilian had requested that his steering column be lengthened for the same reason. Things still weren't brilliant: 'My car reacts a bit nervously on this kind of surface. It stems from the special aerodynamics but it's also got to do with a difficulty in the suspension.'

Interviewed for the BBC, he told Murray Walker: 'We are here, this third round, the European season starting now, starting from zero. So basically our championship starts here, fourteen races, not sixteen. It's not a comfortable position to be in, but that's the reality and the team is conscious about the challenge. We have to ... improve our car's performance.'

In the paddock was Alain Prost, paying a visit to his most recent employers and attending his first Grand Prix of the year.

Senna had seemed in reflective mood all weekend, even before the tragic events of Saturday.

The day before he had recorded a lap of Imola, complete with commentary, for the benefit of French television, for whom Prost was commentating.

As he exited the chicane before the pits to start his lap, his first remark before he blasted towards Tamburello was,

'A special hello to my ... to our dear friend Alain. We all miss you.'

In the two seasons of Senna's career in which he wasn't racing against Alain Prost, his resolve definitely seemed to falter. This may seem like anathema to the hordes of fans who believe he never gave up, but there is an element of truth in it. Senna often spoke of his struggle to find motivation, especially when his cars were not as competitive as others. He openly admitted he missed Prost when he was gone: he couldn't live with him, but he couldn't live without him either.

It was during Friday qualifying that the drama started.

Eurosport commentator Allard Kalff was telling viewers that Senna's qualifying lap was 'good enough for provisional pole so far ... so Ayrton Senna has a 1.22.340 and Michael Schumacher has a one twenty-woooaaaahhh!'.

The cameras cut to the underside of a wrecked Formula 1 car, propped up against the tyre wall.

Exiting the Variante Bassa, the right-left chicane before the pits, the Jordan-Hart of Rubens Barrichello had clipped a kerb and been launched into the air, and the retaining wall, with sickening force.

The car landed on its nose, flipped and landed on its right-hand side. Marshals righted the car with teeth-clenching gusto, the young Brazilian's head juddering about like a punching bag. He was out cold.

A photograph that appeared in that week's *Autosport* captures the surreal moment just before the Jordan strikes the wall: still level but four feet above the ground, the perfect height to clear the tyres that were supposed to absorb the impact of such accidents, Barrichello is holding his hands in front of his face.

When he came round in the medical centre, the first person he saw was Senna. Eight years before, in the same Brazilian TV interview in which Senna had been ribbed for crying, a 14-year-old Barrichello had appeared in a video link and expressed admiration for the elder man. Now Senna was once again in tears as he watched his protégé and friend regain consciousness. He was largely unhurt, incredibly, but he was out of action for the rest of the weekend. Unfortunately F1's luck was about to run out.

The 32-year-old Austrian Roland Ratzenberger was in his first season of Grand Prix racing with the fledgeling Simtek team, also newcomers. The MTV-sponsored cars of Ratzenberger and teammate David Brabham were no great shakes and were to be found, as one might expect, towards the back of the grid.

Nevertheless Roland was a happy man. He had enjoyed fleeting fame in the 1980s having made a memorable appearance on British breakfast show *TV-am* alongside Roland Rat, and competed in a race which ended with the puppet rodent sabotaging his opponent's car. This had raised his profile in the UK, but it was in Japan that he enjoyed success in Formula 3000 before finally realising his dream of making it to the top tier.

Twenty minutes into final qualifying on Saturday 30 April, the TV cameras suddenly switched to the wreck of Ratzenberger's Simtek sliding towards the Tosa hairpin, his crash helmet lolling around in the cockpit. The director hadn't captured the start of the crash, but it had evidently started at the fastest part of the circuit, the 200mph Villeneuve kink.

It didn't need a man of Sid Watkins' expertise to see that this looked bad. In the Williams pit, Senna was glued to the monitors. He was as incredulous as anyone else.

Roland was taken to hospital but he had suffered catastrophic head injuries. His front wing had apparently failed just when he needed the kit most and impact with the wall had inflicted a severe basal skull fracture. He was pronounced dead soon after arrival, aged 33.

Keith Sutton described how the crash affected him:

> I was in the motorhome just before he went out [for his fatal run]. I know I worked with Senna for three years, and it took him three years to get to F1, but it took Roland ten. Roland never gave up. He'd worked really hard to get there on very little money. We were based in Towcester, near Silverstone. We had a lot of drivers come to our little office, our little terraced house. Roland lived close by and he was always popping in, and I got to know him quite well. He went over to Japan and raced and did very well and earned lots of money. Then he finally got his break to do F1. That affected me more. On Sunday I was in a bit of a daze, because no one had ever died at a race circuit where I'd been photographing before.

Keith's mood was reflected everywhere else in the paddock, not least in the Williams garage. The world knew how deeply Senna had been affected by the accident that befell Martin Donnelly four years before, and had seen the efforts he went to to assist his fellow drivers if they were in trouble. He commandeered a safety car to take him to the scene of the crash, though he was reprimanded for this, to his disgust: a man had just died and he was getting dragged into petty squabbles.

Senna then went to speak to his close friend Sid Watkins, who told him that the outlook for the popular Austrian was not good. Senna cried on the Prof's shoulder and Watkins said to him that if he was so disturbed by what he had seen then he should quit and go fishing.

Watkins remembers:

> He thought a great deal before he answered. A minute or
> more. He was always like that. If you asked a difficult
> question, there was always a very long silence – he'd never
> come up with a rapid response, which he might regret.
> Eventually he said that he couldn't not race, in effect.
> There was no particular explanation, but I believe he felt
> trapped by every aspect of his life at that time. I honestly
> think he would have liked to step back; that was the
> impression I'd been getting for a while.

> He'd had a difficult time in his last year with McLaren,
> and then the two races he'd done with Williams had gone
> badly: in Brazil, he'd made a mistake, and spun. At Aida,
> he was shoved off at the first corner. He was very upset
> about those races – he'd just changed teams, and he was
> having more problems than he'd had before. I think
> there's no doubt that he felt very much pressured that
> he had to win at Imola.

Senna opted to get out of the paddock as quickly as possible.
Tellingly he asked Jo Ramirez to organise it, rather than anyone
from Williams. He went back to his hotel room and phoned
Adriane, again sobbing bitterly about what had happened. He
did not calm down until much later when he went for a meal
with Brazilian friends.

In the drivers' briefing the next morning Senna, Schumacher,
Berger agreed to act as directors for the reformed Grand Prix
Drivers' Association, an organisation that had been formed in
1961 but had long since fallen by the wayside. Complacency had
set in and now was the time for action.

Senna started the race from his third consecutive pole position. He had set his time on Friday and had not run at all on

Saturday following Ratzenberger's crash, a move echoed by the Benetton team, but had still beaten Schumacher into second as he had done all year so far.

Before getting into his car he gave Gerhard Berger a wry smile as the *tifosi* greeted the Tannoy announcement of their hero's name with rapturous cheers.

When he was strapped into his cockpit, much was made of the fact that he sat in his car with his helmet off, suggesting to some that he was feeling uneasy.

Senna once said: 'People always think the start of a race is something terrible, that your heart beats like mad, that your brain is about to explode, but it's a totally unreal moment, like a dream, like entering another world', but he looked nothing more than distracted, and very much in this world, surrounded by his own earthly concerns.

Alas, his concerns were multiplied five seconds into the start of the race.

Finn JJ Lehto had been absent for the first two races with a broken neck but had made an amazing, and impressive, return to the Benetton team by qualifying fifth. But at the green light he stalled and was rammed by the Lotus of Pedro Lamy, which had started eight rows further back and had gained some serious momentum. Neither driver was hurt, although that was more than could be said for nine members of the crowd who were hit by the flying debris from the two cars.

The safety car was immediately deployed and picked up Senna, who had converted pole into the lead. Some reckoned the race should have been stopped while the start–finish straight was cleaned properly, but the black Opel Vectra was deemed sufficient by the powers that be.

A family saloon was an unlikely choice: the safety car should of course be slow enough to ensure the safety of marshals and drivers out of their cars, but at the same time it needs to be quick enough to keep the expensive machinery behind it working properly. F1 cars, like their drivers, do not like going too slowly and what was essentially a Vauxhall Cavalier was, irrefutably, doing just that.

The Vectra meandered while the tyre pressures and ride heights of all twenty-three cars behind it dropped. Senna was visibly impatient, pulling up alongside the car to express his frustration.

At the end of lap 5, Williams radioed Senna to let him know that the green flag was about to be given. He acknowledged the message with probably the last words he ever uttered.

'When they released the cars, Ayrton went by my medical car [parked at the chicane, before the pit straight] like a bat out of hell,' recalls Watkins. 'I'm not given to premonitions, but when he came past me, I said to Mario Casoni, my driver, "I've got a feeling there's going to be a f*cking awful accident …".'

On the first flying lap, a shower of sparks flew from the underside of the Williams as it jinked through Tamburello, Senna building a gap over the pursuing Schumacher behind.

And then, on lap seven, twelve minutes since he had left his grid position, Ayrton Senna went into the infamous left-hand kink for the last time.

———

Looking at the Imola circuit on Google Maps in early 2012, one might have noticed that the stretch of tarmac that runs through Tamburello was labelled 'Via John Fitzgerald Kennedy'. It is no longer, presumably because it was incorrect, but it would have been poetic if true. Senna and JFK have obvious parallels: both charismatic men who achieved worldwide fame at a young age, became arguably the most widely-known practitioners of their discipline and both died a premature death in very public circumstances. Everyone of a certain age remembers what they were doing when JFK was shot; every F1 fan recalls where they were when Senna died.

What caused the crash that killed arguably the sport's greatest driver will both never be known and never stop being subject of debate.

The Italian authorities treated Senna's death as manslaughter. They liked their theory that the car's modified steering column had snapped and stuck to their guns through retrial after retrial, no matter how implausible the scenario sounded as more evidence came to light: evidence such as the fact that Senna was still steering the car right up to the impact. The steering column was certainly broken when the wheel was pulled from the cockpit, but it had, after all, just been involved in a crash at three-figure speed. This is the explanation still trotted out by the armies of pro-Senna fans and conspiracy theorists who flood the Internet with their ill-informed ramblings. The comments section under every YouTube video about Senna will somehow feature a lengthy debate about his death, even if the video in question is nothing to do with the event itself.

For the men most closely associated with the crash, the Williams trio of Frank Williams, technical director Patrick Head and the car's designer Adrian Newey, these were miserable times.

'The little hair I had all fell out in the aftermath', Newey told the The Guardian in 2011.

> So it changed me physically. It was dreadful. Both Patrick Head and myself separately asked ourselves whether we wanted to continue in racing.

> For the whole team it was incredibly difficult. I remember the day after the race was a bank holiday Monday and some of us came in to try and trawl though the data and work out what happened. They were dark weeks. The honest truth is that no one will ever know exactly what happened.

'If you look at the camera shots, especially from Michael Schumacher's following car, the car didn't understeer off the track. It oversteered which is not consistent with a steering column failure. The rear of the car stepped out and all the data suggests that happened. Ayrton then corrected that by going to 50% throttle which would be consistent with trying to reduce the rear stepping out and then, half-a-second later, he went hard on the brakes.

The question then is why did the rear step out? The car bottomed much harder on that second lap which again appears to be unusual because the tyre pressure should have come up by then – which leaves you expecting that the right rear tyre probably picked up a puncture from debris on the track. If I was pushed into picking out a single most likely cause that would be it.

There is, of course, a more unpalatable explanation.

I am convinced that he made a mistake,' said Damon Hill in 2004, 'but many people will never believe that he could.'

Why not? He made many mistakes in his career. I have listened to and read endless theories about why, or how, he could have crashed on such a 'simple' corner like Tamburello.

No one other than Ayrton Senna and me know what it was like to drive that car, through that corner, in that race, on that day, on cold tyres.

He was identified with pushing to the limit and beyond. He would often prefer to crash into his opponent rather than be defeated. It was not the fault of anyone else that he kept his foot flat when he could have lifted.

> These opinions are sacrilege in the world of driving gods. Ayrton was a great driver and a man with enormous humanity [but] he was not a god. He was as frail and vulnerable as you or I.

Hill is not the type of man who willingly invites controversy and he must have been bracing himself as he wrote these words for the *Times*, but he is a man whose opinions cannot be dismissed lightly.

Remember, Senna had spun the Williams into retirement in Brazil five weeks before, at a spot in which he never misjudged. He spun during qualifying at Aida and then made a poor start the next day which led to his first-corner crash. A driver, no matter how good he is, is only as good as his equipment and Senna was no different.

Senna hadn't made many mistakes during his career but that didn't mean he had not made a single one. After qualifying for Monaco in 1988 he was responsible for one of F1's most bewildering errors when he slammed into the Armco. His crash at Peraltada in qualifying for the 1991 Mexican Grand Prix happened because he attempted to take the curve in a higher gear than normal, and he simply lost control of his McLaren.

Grand Prix cars are inherently difficult to drive, even the good ones. There is not a driver alive who has not made a major mistake at some juncture. It just might very well be possible that Senna happened to make one at the worst possible moment.

Nigel Roebuck agrees: 'My own belief has always been that Ayrton, in a Williams FW16 still far from honed, simply went into Tamburello at a speed, and on a line, which the car, for whatever reason, could not sustain. At this, the third race of the season, he was without a point, and driving out of his skin to stay ahead of Schumacher's faster Benetton.'

Is this a valid point?

Ron Dennis doesn't think so. 'There are people who would claim that his pursuit of Michael in the Benetton was overly aggressive because of the necessity to compensate for the inadequacies of his car. But I think that's nonsense: it's just people trying to rewrite the script. Simple fact is that Ayrton almost certainly suffered a car failure which caused the accident and it was one of those things.'

Of course, none of this really matters. What was already a desperately sad weekend with the death of Ratzenberger the day before had become even more heartrending.

The race was restarted, and Michael Schumacher won. But nobody cared. Murray Walker spoke for everyone watching when he said 'I think as far as everybody is concerned, the finish of the 1994 San Marino Grand Prix cannot come a second too soon. There will be a lot of thankful hearts that this GP is finishing, and I think that's the first time I've ever said that.'

Over in the US, Senna's death was announced at the Talladega Superspeedway during the NASCAR Winston Cup round. The drivers completed two silent laps in tribute.

Race winner Dale Earnhardt, who would himself perish in a racing accident seven years later, said 'I want to send our thoughts and prayers to the family of Ayrton Senna and all his fans. He was a great racer and it's a shame to see him go like he did.'

Damon Hill would bravely rise to the challenge of leading the Williams team, just as much as his father Graham had done for Lotus in 1968 after the death of Jim Clark.

The season went on, with further sadness and controversy, until the title was eventually decided in Michael Schumacher's favour after the infamous clash with Hill in Adelaide. The German was quick to acknowledge that if Senna had lived it would probably have been he who was celebrating the championship instead.

At the bottom of the final 1994 standings, just below Roland Ratzenberger, was the almost ephemeral name of Ayrton Senna, as though he had never been there in the first place.

When the medical team had extracted Senna from his wrecked car at the side of the Imola circuit, they found a small Austrian flag which he had intended to wave on the slowing-down lap, as a celebration of his first win for Williams and in remembrance of his fallen comrade. For all his faults, Ayrton Senna was a gentleman to the end.

Bibliography

BOOKS

Berger, Gerhard, *Na Reta de Chegada* (Editora Globo, year unknown)

Byrne, Tommy and Hughes, Mark (*Crashed and Byrned,* Corinthian, 2009)

Folley, Malcolm, *Senna versus Prost* (Arrow Books, 2009)

Mansell, Nigel, *My Autobiography* (HarperCollins, 1996)

Rubython, Tom, *The Life of Senna* (Business F1 Books, 2004)

Various authors, *Autosport Legends: Ayrton Senna* (Haymarket Publishing, 2011)

Ward, Pete, *Gods Behaving Badly* (SCM Press, 2011)

Williams, Richard, *The Death of Ayrton Senna* (Bloomsbury, 1995)

ONLINE

Bulgin, Russell, 'Ayrton Senna: Rally Driver', *Cars and Conversions*, November 1986

Collantine, Keith, '25 years since Ayrton Senna's first F1 win: 1985 Portuguese flashback', f1fanatic.co.uk, 21 April 2010

Cooper, Adam, Transcript of Irvine/Senna conversation as republished by themagicofsenna.com

Cassell, Paul and Pyle, Mike, 'Ayrton Senna – A legend … but not in the garden,' *Get Reading*, 23 June 2011

Crask, Andrew, 'Stunting for Growth, racer.com,' 9 August 2010

Doodson, Mike, 'Memories of Senna', Motor Sport, 2010

Fielding, Noel, 'How Dalí and Senna influenced my Luxury Comedy', *The Guardian Guide*, 21 January 2012

Folley, Malcolm, 'Scorching Schumacher,' *Daily Mail,* 26 May 2012

Fowler, Rich, 'Jo Ramirez and Gerald Donaldson discuss Senna's 1988 Monaco Pole Lap,' motorsportretro.com, 27 May 2011

Hallbery, Andy, Legends: 'Nelson Piquet,' motorsportretro.com, 6 March 2011

Halbery, Andy, 'Martin Donnelly crash (Parts 1–4),' motorsportretro.com, 22 August 2011

Hayward, Paul, 'Cinematic Senna drives home the joy of a pre-corporate sporting age,' *The Observer*, 12 June 2011

Jenkinson, Denis, 'The Mind of a Great Racing Driver: An Interview with Ayrton Senna,' reproduced by sportscars.tv

McRae, Donald, 'Ayrton Senna's death "changed me physically", says Adrian Newey,' *The Guardian*, 16 May 2011

Medland, Chris, 'Senna Reigns Supreme,' espn.com, 24 June 2011

Roebuck, Nigel, 'Ayrton Senna, by Alain Prost,' *Motor Sport*, 1 October 1998, reproduced by ayrton-senna.co.uk

Schuler, Oskar, 'Where were you when Senna nearly killed Prost?,' prostfan.com, September 2004

Strang, Simon, 'Why The Senna Legend Still Stands Strong,' autosport.com, 3 June 2011

Straw, Edd, 'Ron Dennis on Ayrton Senna,' autosport.com, 3 June 2011

Tremayne, David, 'Lewis Hamilton: World leader driven to get back to front,' *The Independent*, 22 March 2009

UNKNOWN/VARIOUS AUTHORS

Ayrton Senna: In His Own Words, espn.com, 21 March 2010

It was thirty years ago today …Keith Sutton Remembers Ayrton Senna's first car victory, sutton-images.com, March 8 2011

Hill: Senna was at fault, bbc.co.uk, 20 April 2004

Mosley: Senna Should Have Been Excluded in 1990, AtlasF1, 21 February 2002

Remembering Ayrton Senna's first car win, YallaF1, 15 March 2011

Top Five of 2011: Formula 1, motorsportretro.com, 12 January 2012

Plus an entire swathe of race reports from the Autosport archives from 1984–1994, written by Nigel Roebuck, Jeff Hutchinson, and Joe Saward, including the reports of the following races:

- 1985 Portuguese Grand Prix
- 1986 Brazilian Grand Prix
- 1986 Spanish Grand Prix
- 1986 Canadian Grand Prix
- 1986 Detroit Grand Prix
- 1988 Canadian Grand Prix
- 1988 British Grand Prix
- 1989 Japanese Grand Prix
- 1990 Japanese Grand Prix
- 1991 Brazilian Grand Prix
- 1991 Japanese Grand Prix
- 1993 European Grand Prix
- 1994 San Marino Grand Prix

I have also used numerous quotes from the *Ask Nigel* feature on autosport.com. This has been a truly valuable resource.